The Relationship Marketing Model

Instant Strategies to Increase Your Local Marketing & Gain Lifetime Customers

by

Justin D. Taylor

ISBN-13: 978-0615541860 (Alliant)

ISBN-10: 0615541860

First Printing, 2012

Second Printing, 2015

Printed in the United States of America

Income Disclaimer

This document contains business strategies, marketing methods and other business advice that, regardless of my own results and experience, may not produce the same results (or any results) for you. I make absolutely no guarantee, expressed or implied, that by following the advice below you will make any money or improve current profits, as there are several factors and variables that come into play regarding any given business.

Primarily, results will depend on the nature of the product or business model, the conditions of the marketplace, the experience of the individual, and situations and elements that are beyond your control.

As with any business endeavor, you assume all risk related to investment and money based on your own discretion and at your own potential expense.

The Relationship Marketing Model

Instant Strategies to Increase Your
Local Marketing & Create
Lifetime Customers

Dedication

This book is dedicated to all those that have believed in me. My parents and family and to my friends that always knew I had and still have the potential to do great things.

I also need to thank my business partner Brent, because without him, this book, the Relationship Marketing Model, and much of the content found inside, would probably never have materialized.

Table of Contents

Foreword

Do you know what the most profitable skill is for running a small business?

It's not keeping the shelves stocked. It's not managing employees. It's not even having a good product.

No. The most important skill is *marketing your business*. Why? Well, the only time you can bring money into your business is if you *sell* something. You can't stock the shelves unless you have money to buy the stuff to put on the shelves.

And you can't pay your employees unless you have money coming in the business from selling stuff. A good product might as well be a piece of junk in a box if nobody knows it exists.

That's where marketing comes in. It's how you communicate to the public that you have a good product, that you offer a good consumer experience and that they should buy stuff from you, rather than one of your competitors.

Marketing is also the most misunderstood skill on the planet. Poor Marketing is perhaps why 65% of new businesses close their doors after 2 years, and over 85% of businesses don't make it 8 years before going under.

Most of your competition simply does not understand how to do marketing properly…to bring in amazing results in little to no time. So just knowing a few simple things will put you at a great advantage. Marketing is the heart of your business and everything else is built around that heart to protect it and make it function even better.

In the land of the blind, the person with one eye is KING!

You are about to learn the 12 Steps of the Relationship Marketing Model, along with the 7 most powerful – and profitable – marketing strategies that you can start using today to become the "king" in your own local marketplace within 3 months time.

You have right now, in your hands, information that could change your life forever. Use it and profit from it.

All the best,

Justin Taylor

Introduction

Before you begin reading this book, I wanted to be sure you understood a couple of things about, what this book is and what it is not.

What this book is not. This book is not a "how to" build a business book. It isn't even about what types of businesses you might want to consider building. This book is not an attempt to cover each topic presented in full and complete detail.

What this book is. This book is quite simply, a guide to creating a proper and firm foundation for your business, whether you have been in business for dozens of years or you are just thinking about starting one. This book is just presenting some very simple but often misunderstood concepts, which have volumes of information written about them already. This book is an overview of concepts, mixed with some very real ideas that can and will improve your business.

The information presented in this book is relevant and timely, and in many ways, evergreen. Evergreen simply means, that the concepts are just as new and fresh today as they will be in 5 or 10 years. Evergreen information is timeless information.

If you have been to business school, I hope you will recognize the concepts and this will be a reminder and a guide to you. If you have not been to business school, I hope this book will fill in a few of the missing gaps for you and help you get a better idea of how to build a successful business. I hope it will inspire you to reach new heights and not make some of the more classic mistakes that cause businesses to fail.

The Relationship Marketing Model is separated into two primary sections. The first 5 steps are the foundation, while the next 7 steps are areas of focus that need to be included in that foundation.

You may visually see, the Relationship Marketing Model at: www.RelationshipMarketingModel.com.

In the Beginning...

What you are about to read is the culmination of many years of research and experience. Through a lot of schools and more classes than I would like to admit, I spent a lot of time finding out what didn't work. With multiple failed businesses and an inability to find any sort of happiness toward working for someone else. No matter what I did, I always had some sort of a side business, something that compelled me to want to do more.

One day after several years of planning and working, my business partner and I were joking with each other about programs that are designed to help people. We were talking about things we had read about them and how they are often a huge marketing gimmick. As a marketer this got me thinking.

One of the best articles that you can write has always been to base it on a list.

<u>5 Things You Always Do Before You Go on a Date.</u>

<u>7 Top Reasons to Not Buy a Car.</u>

<u>Top 10 Ways to Start a Business on a Shoestring Budget.</u>

You use a specific number that is easy for people to remember and you make points about it. It catches people's attention.

There are also certain numbers that you use that work better than others and there is a fine line between too few or too many. Why not use 12 as a number and create a 12 step business/marketing rehab program. Something to save people from themselves, that addresses many of the top reasons why businesses fail. Those reasons are usually around marketing, advertising, and just general lack of having any specific plans for success.

That was the inspiration for the book you are now reading. It was surprising to me how simple each of the 12 steps or points were to come up with. After sharing it with my business partner, we decided that we needed a unique way of describing the biggest problem so many businesses have and this required us to create a new word.

The main purpose originally was to create a simple report. So using bits and pieces of Latin and some assumptions to make the point, the word Praeconititus was born. More will be discussed in the next chapter about what this really means and why it is important. But quite simply Praeconititus is a "No-Plan Marketing" disease related to advertising without a plan.

Most businesses tend to do the shotgun approach, where they plan out an advertising plan, with some advertiser or agency, but they don't necessarily have a very effective marketing plan. In fact if they have a marketing plan, it may not be based on a strong business plan.

This general lack of planning is a huge problem. It's a huge waste of money and businesses truly can't afford to keep doing this. Especially in times of economic hardship. Yet many persist in doing it, day after day, month after month. It's important that all business activities are included in a marketing plan and during business school and from experience I realized that most small to even mid-size businesses don't seem to include everything in a marketing plan.

Generally only very large fortune 500 corporations spend the time and effort required to properly plan and then implement those plans. But consider that they spend hundreds of thousands of dollars on consultants, efficiency experts, specialists of other kinds, and training and personal and professional coaches. They understand the need to plan.

Of these types of companies, there are even less that are highly efficient and have truly eliminated much of the waste. A couple that come to mind are Southwest Airlines and USAA. The struggle that those at the top deal with more than anything else is the fine line that exists between the potential for waste in time, money, and energy to actually create and implement these plans, and that which is considered valuable.

Are all of these top companies perfect? Not by any stretch of the imagination. Many still have efficiency issues, as a result of too much internal planning and that creates red tape, which makes them slow to react to major changes. Many still have 'Relationship' issues with clients, suppliers, and employees. I mentioned both Southwest Airlines and USAA, because they have stellar relationships with their customers, with award winning customer service departments, and they manage to have a great deal of loyalty.

Let's also be clear that I'm not saying money is everything. There are many aspects of what should or needs to be done as a business that are hard to quantify financially. For example, the true value of your brand image. How much is it really worth?

Yes, there are formulas that can help you determine what your brand value is, but ultimately those calculations are based on speculation and guessing, and the value of the brand is only what someone is willing to pay for it. Sort of like a fine piece of art; nobody knows exactly what it is worth, until someone speaks up with his or her pocketbook.

The Silo

What my business partner and I created is a holistic approach to solving business problems, instead of the antiquated traditional silo approach that most businesses use. It is common in business, to look at everything in silos.

What do we mean by Silo? That means, we see a problem and then we go out and find one person or company to solve that one problem.

Say the problem is in HR. You have employees that are unhappy and keep leaving the company to find other jobs. You even give pay raises, but for some reason that doesn't seem to help. Then you realize that you are losing lots of money in HR due to the constant turnover, so you decide to do an internal survey. In this survey you find that your employees are not happy with their benefits, they don't think the ones they have are useful and they don't feel like they have enough. Now you know that money is only part of the equation, so as a business, you go out and find a good HR company to provide some solutions to your problems.

This saves you thousands of dollars on your balance sheet. The HR company then creates a whole new benefits package, that seem on the surface to solve many of the problems. But when or how often does your HR company or division really look at your entire Business or Marketing plan to see how the new benefit plans may directly affect other parts of the business? Not very often, if ever.

The silo approach tends to neglect all other aspects of any given business and doesn't view every part of it with the symbiotic relationship that really exists. Everything you do in your businesses has an effect on every other part of your business. It's like one giant living organism that must be treated in a way that focuses on the whole and not just the sum of it's parts. For years, it worked to just solve problems as they happened and to piecemeal everything. But in a time when efficiency in operations and saving money is so important, these old methods no longer work.

After creating the 12 Steps, I recognized the fact that not everyone would easily see or understand how the pieces really fit together or what the ultimate goal really should be. So I took this process one step further and created the Relationship Marketing Model, which is more a visual representation of the all the steps. It shows why having a strong foundation is so important. It shows where each piece fits and how they interact with every other step in the model. More importantly it expresses the most vital of all the concepts that has been reborn in the last 5-10 years; relationship marketing.

Relationships are key to everything you do as a business. Not only the relationship with your customers, as much of social media focuses on, but also the relationships you have with employees and vendors too. What are you doing to empower your employees? Do you have a relationship that makes them feel wanted or needed?

Every stake holder in a business has a vital relationship with the overall success of a business and the more you focus on those relationships the more successful your business will really be.

What is Praeconititus?

First, let's define what Praecontitis is. "Prae" comes from the Latin, meaning pre or before. "Con" from the Latin "contactus" which is literally you the contact. Put those together and you have the more literal meaning of Marketing, which is planning to put something 'before a contact'. [2]

Praeconititus is a highly contagious virus, that can eat at your business by spending more and more money on shotgun advertising... marketing without a plan. Many Businesses have this disease, but don't see the signs until it is too late... another way to say it is, "no-plan" marketing.

The whole purpose of any business is to eventually get some product or service or idea in front of some person or business (a contact, if you will) that will then take some sort of action on it, usually in the form of buying, acquiring or using.

Now ask yourself: Are the Advertising Cons, Preying upon you?

It is very possible that they have at one point in time, nearly everyone has been a victim.

Without knowing anything about you or your business; I can with a great deal of confidence say, that at one point or another you have spent money or time on something that would be considered 'Advertising' or 'Marketing' related and you didn't consider the overall long term plan.

You probably didn't even look at your business or marketing plans (if you even have updated ones) to see if what you were doing fit into your overall goals.

It's possible that you even bought into some emotional hype or peer pressure, that everyone else was doing it, so why shouldn't you? (*For example, when you got health insurance or any other benefits for you or your employees, did you consider your ROI?*)

In some cases, the things you did might have worked and could have resulted in some positive result. Or maybe it made some of your employees a little happier or there are numerous other positive things that could have happened.

If you have ever purchased or acquired anything, without considering your Marketing or Business Plan first, then that could be your first contact with the 'bug'. The first time you spent money and then justified it because it was successful is another. At this point it became easier and easier to just do things, because it seemed right. It made it easier to make important on-the-fly decisions, without first considering the long-term effects of those decisions.

This is just another form of gambling.

Think about it, if you have never gambled in your life and then one day you decide to gamble with some friends and you get really lucky and win something. That feeling of winning is pretty amazing and there is even a little bit of a rush when you do. Then you think, that was really easy, so without a lot of experience or thought, you do it again. You have some wins and some losses, but ultimately you have a lot of fun and you walk away with a little money or some prizes or something else of value.

Then because you didn't really have any plan or any experience, you start putting more and more money down, justifying every loss you have, with something like, "I'm just testing to learn what the best way is, because I'm still learning." Alright, be honest, have you ever had that thought in your mind when it comes to your advertising?

You consider it the price of your education and you think in your mind, that you are actually getting better at it, and maybe you are, but the odds are always stacked against you.

But your business or the way you run your business is no Casino. You are placing bets with some business decision, in the hopes that this one might be the one that makes the big time. Every time it does, you get excited and want to find ways to repeat that success. Every time it doesn't you justify the losses with some excuse, until they become excessive.

Don't misunderstand me, testing in advertising and in any marketing related activity is necessary. It's a part of the process. But my point here is, does all that testing and all those campaigns really fit into your overall goals? Does every other marketing related activity, that isn't just advertising, fit into your overall goals?

Do you really want to 'gamble' your business?

When was the last time any of your advertising reps asked you about your marketing plan?

Did they help make sure it was complete and met all your actual goals?

I bet your answer to both of these questions was "No" or "I don't think they ever did ask me that." It's pretty common that you will find advertising vultures or 'cons' that want nothing more than to have you spend money in a shotgun style approach on anything they are selling. They may be kind enough to create an 'Advertising Plan', but if that plan is not based off of an effective Marketing Plan, that is based on a solid Business plan, then you are a victim!

Advertising is a huge part of Marketing and although they are not the same thing, ultimately all forms of marketing requires some form of advertising as the end result. People need to know about you and what you are offering or they won't ever take advantage of it.

How can you avoid Praecontitis?

While the Relationship Marketing Model, will help you find a way to break your addiction to wasting money on Marketing. These 12 steps are just the beginning and they are not the same for every business or every person in every situation.

These steps are just an outline of the top 12 things every business needs to do, including yours, if you expect to break your addiction to wasting your marketing dollars and to help more effectively focus your spending.

As you progress through the following 12 steps, you should notice how each one builds upon the step before it. It's very important to commit to do each step in order, or to at least cover and plan for each step, even if it doesn't appear to be a focus for your particular business right now. Each step is important to your marketing efforts and disregarding any of them, will lead to wasting more money.

Don't be a Victim!!

<u>Following are the 12 Steps of the Relationship Marketing Model:</u>

Step 1: You are not an expert at everything. Admit it!

Regardless of whether you have a new business or one that has been established for many years, the fact is you still aren't an expert at everything and there is always room for improvement. Discover your strengths, so you can focus all your energy in those areas and find other 'experts' to do everything else. Even as a sole proprietor, you can't and definitely shouldn't even try to do everything alone.

So you already have an accountant and a lawyer and a friend down the street that does all your printing. That's not enough!

Do you have someone that handles all your marketing? What are you doing to avoid Praecontitus?

As you have read, more businesses fail because of not understanding how to market, than any other reason.

Most businesses start because of the passion of an individual or a couple of individuals. That passion could be to solve a problem. It could be because an employer quit listening to ideas. It might be just to solve a general problem or due to some innovation or change in policy.

Whatever the reason, there is usually a passion that drives someone to take the leap and start a new business. As a result, most business owners are 'experts' at something. There is at least one area, which they are better than most people, an area that people will likely want to come to them to get answers.

A question I like to ask people, out of natural curiosity more than anything, is "What is your passion?" and "Do you have an area that you feel you are an expert?"

As a business owner or even a future business owner, there is a tendency to wear more hats than you should. Most of the time it is out of necessity, but on rare occasion it is out of desire.

Regardless of whether you have a new business or one that has been established for many years, the fact is you still aren't an expert at everything and there is always room for improvement. Discover your strengths, so you can focus all your energy in those areas and find other 'experts' to do everything else. Even as a sole proprietor, you can't and definitely shouldn't even try to do everything alone.

Why is this step so crucial to your business success?

It's important because if you aren't willing to ask for help, then you aren't going to be willing to accept it. If you aren't willing to listen to advice or to the wisdom of other experts, then why should the advice even be given? That is a waste of both your time and the time of the other experts.

It's not uncommon to find sole-proprietors or very new and small businesses that are stuck in a conundrum of what to do and how to get to that next level after start up. The conundrum is this.

On the one hand, they may have sacrificed every penny they have, including their credit and reputation with family and friends and their time. They have put their heart and soul into starting something new and great, for whatever reason. It's their baby; it's their sacrifice, because they took the risks.

Now, in order to get what they need, they want someone else to take risks with them. So they are looking for people, ideas or anything they can get their hands on, in order to figure out how to move to the next level.

But this is where they experience the conflict. They have an internal need to maintain power and control over their so-called 'brain child', while also having the need for assistance because they are not experts at everything. They must learn to release the reigns of control and take yet, another risk, that someone else will treat their business as important as they do. They must overcome the emotional connection they have and let others with no emotional connection, assist them in their growth.

The sooner you find a way to separate yourself from your business emotionally, the sooner your business will grow exponentially.

Step 2: Treat your business like a real business and not like a job.

Regardless of the size of your business, it's important and necessary that you treat your business like the company that it is. A common problem among smaller business owners and sole-proprietors is their business becomes a job. Investing thousands of dollars and years of your time to just buy a job isn't a very wise investment. You need to be running your business, instead of your business running you.

Being committed to the success of your business and being forced to make choices that have you hating what you do, are two completely different things. When you are completely tied to your business or left to the whims of every little thing in the market, because it's your 'job', it becomes easy to work 60- 80 or more hours per week and then justify it, even when you aren't being paid for it.

It is true that running a business can mean making a lot of sacrifices with your time and money, because there is risk involved. But the sooner you recognize and treat your business as a business, the sooner you will have the freedom and independence that comes from being a business owner. You can be committed to a job, but with a normal 9-5 type job working for someone else, you can usually just quit anytime you want and get another one if things become unbearable or you need a change in your life. To make this point, statistically speaking, on average people change jobs every 5 years.

With a business, it may be that your entire financial, emotional, and family life is tied to the success or failure of it.

Being a small business owner is a lifestyle; it's not something you casually commit to, until something better comes along.

How do you solve this problem?

You can't wear all the hats and you want your business to be more than just a job, so it is important that you consider all the options for filling the needs of your business. The answer to this question is quite simple; you outsource it.

Outsourcing is about leveraging your time and your talents. Sometimes outsourcing makes more sense than hiring someone to do a job internally. But even hiring someone internally is a form of 'outsourcing' tasks that you should not be focusing your time and efforts on. Whether you hire or contract, inside or outside of your company, is something that only you can decide. As you will soon see, this is where having a plan is so important.

When do you outsource?

The immediate answer is as soon as possible. The sooner you begin outsourcing tasks, the sooner you are free to focus on the more important aspects of your business. Perhaps it is doing what you love most, like making something or it might be that you need to focus on revenue generation. Ultimately, only you, and your plan (*which we will discuss more in the next few chapters*) can decide the answer to this question.

What should you outsource?

This is another question that has a lot of variables to consider. For some, it may be that they started a business because they were good at something that they really loved. For others, they may have invented something or came up with a new idea or concept. Then there are those of you that started a business simply to have more freedom in your lives or out of necessity, because of downsizing or some other factor outside of your control. In these cases, it may be more about what in your business makes you the most money. The smaller the business, the more important it is to focus on how you earn the most revenue.

But just as you would hire an outside attorney, or accountant, or even online marketing coach, you also may want to consider outsourcing other tasks to other qualified experts/specialists.

There are many tasks that you might consider:

- Complicated Tasks That Require a Certain Level of Expertise.
- Too Costly To Do On Your Own and Less Expensive For Someone Else To Do For You.
- Easy But Time-Consuming Tasks.
- Tasks You Know and Understand, But Hate Doing.
- Tasks That Do Nothing to Increase Your Bottom Line, But Someone Must Still Do Them.

If you are prone to micro-manage or you are a 'control freak', (*and you know who you are*) this is a good time to learn to let go. The sooner you learn to let go of those things that do not make money for you or that simply are not the reason you started a business, the sooner you will have a business, that you run and that does not run you.

Always ask yourself, who is in control, you or your business?

Step 3: Have, know, reevaluate or write your business plan.

At all stages of a businesses life, a business plan is both important and necessary. This is the step where you review your business plan. If you don't have one, take the time to create it. Re-evaluate your value proposition, re-assess your competition and examine your operations.

When was the last time you did a full reevaluation of your business plan? What, you haven't... Why not? How do you know if you are achieving the goals you set out to achieve when you started your business? What new goals have you set in the last 3-5 years? If you are a start-up or newer business, do you need or perhaps want start-up capital?

Regardless of what stage you are in, you need an updated relevant business plan that has clear goals for yourself or your investors and employees, if you have them. A Business Plan answers the what, why, and sometimes where of your business.

There are two primary types of business plans. The financial business plan and the working business plan.

The difference between the two is a considerable one.

A financial business plan has one single purpose, to raise money. Everything in the plan is written to that end. There is research, background information, historical data, and a lot of numerical data that may be very forward thinking. In some cases this may be for a brand new business idea, that has never seen a profit and has zero financial records. In other cases, it may be for a business that has been running for a short or even longer period of time, and there is a lot more historical data.

In either case, all of this data is used to support forward projections that will inspire investors into wanting to give you money.

The other type of plan is the working business plan. This is the plan that most small business owners fail to create. They go out and get funding and then they run their business not thinking about what goals they might have. They figure they have a business plan and it never needs to be updated. Not realizing that this is part of the goal setting for a business. Sometimes a business plan may not change hardly at all, if at all, over time. But it is important that mission statements, goals, and values be looked at to validate whether they are still important or even on track.

This is a step that often needs to be done, just so that newer employees or managers know what the short and long-term strategies of the business are moving forward.

A response I often hear is that, the business plan is proprietary and the business does not want to share it with anyone, but investors. My response is always the same. You do not have to show them the entire plan, such as every financial or proprietary detail. Besides this is a working business plan anyway. It is important that you share other data, such as your goals, projections, mission statements, and values, and that you get any managers or supervisors you may have all on the same page.

Some businesses, usually larger ones, incorporate many of these values and tools from the business plan, into an employee handbook. If you have a number of employees, then it makes sense to go this route. If you do not, then there are other ways to pass the same information along to those that need to know and understand it, on a regular and frequent basis.

When I was in the Air Force, I remember my supervisors hating the number of meetings they went to on a regular basis. There was a planning meeting for a deployment, a planning meeting for the shop, a quarterly report and separate planning meeting, a meeting with the commander, a meeting with... and the list always went on and on. But what the military understood with many of those meetings is that everyone had to be on the same page. Everyone in the unit had to understand the mission and anytime there was a change to that mission or a change to a statement, it was important to update all senior leadership and then have them pass it down through the ranks.

I am not going to say that it was always efficient, but I will say that when the system worked, everyone in the unit worked well together and we were able to accomplish a lot, while saving a lot of money and time for both the unit and the taxpayers.

This leads, to one of the most common statements that I hear from people that have worked in the corporate world and then left it, which is that the corporate environment, has too many meetings. They are always in planning mode. They have meetings, and memos for everything.

There is nothing that says that you have to have millions of meetings. You are not required to turn your company into a meeting machine and you do not have to mimic all the things you do not like about a large corporation.

Remember it is your business, you are in control, you decide what the culture of your business will be and how you will approach it.

What is important however, is keeping good communication and making sure everyone in your organization knows what the plan is and how it affects him or her.

Oh, one more thing about business plans. Your business plan does not have to be 60 or even hundreds (yes, there are plans actually that long) of pages long, it only has to be one page. One single page is all it takes to get started. You can easily add to it as you go.

I have three recommendations, two books and a software program. My books came with the software, but even if they don't, you should still consider reading them.

The first book is called '*The Plan As You Go Business Plan*', By Tim Berry. He's the principle author of the software, *Business Plan Pro*. The software will walk even a novice through all the steps of creating a business plan. Tim Berry is also perhaps one of the foremost authorities on Business Plans; he really does know his stuff. The second book with him as an author too is called, '*Hurdle – The Book on Business Planning*.'

Of the hundreds of books written on business plans and business planning these are probably two of the easiest to understand and are two of the most practical books on the subject that I have read. I highly recommend you get these books and read through them if you want to understand how to create a working business plan that will grow with your business. Business planning is not hard to do, if you just understand the basics and you are willing to be patient with the process.

Step 4: Have a written marketing plan, based on your business plan, with well-defined action oriented goals.

You must faithfully stick to your marketing plan and give it time to work.

Wait one second. Did you read that? This is important enough to repeat it again.

You must faithfully stick to your marketing plan and give it time to work. Time is a critical factor in any marketing plan. Any form of marketing or advertising takes time to know whether or not it is working for you. It may take 3-6 months before you can honestly know whether a particular strategy is a complete success or a complete failure. Sometimes the strategy requires a little tweaking, a minor change here or there, but without taking the time to make it work, you will never know if it will work or not.

A thorough marketing plan is the foundation to success in any business. Again, a thorough marketing plan is the foundation to success in any business. As mentioned in the introduction, this is the heart and soul of your business. Marketing is that important. In times of economic upheaval, those small businesses and big businesses alike, that have a solid marketing plan are most likely to be the ones that survive. You can often tell those, which did not have a very good plan and were perhaps successful, by shear luck.

Without a solid marketing plan, it is unlikely that your business will ever achieve any of the goals you set, in your business plan. Please note that the larger your business in size or operations, the more likely it is you could have multiple marketing plans. There are marketing plans for everything. Every product or service you sell, as a business should have a marketing plan specific to the product or service being sold.

Every product you create, every idea you have that might be a product, should first start with some form of a marketing plan, which starts with very thorough and complete research. But you should still have one single primary marketing plan, that governs all areas of your business and is primarily driven by your business plan. This is crucial to long-term success.

Just like with business plans, there are hundreds of books written about marketing plans, or about how to do marketing, and there are dozens of types of marketing. Just to name a few of the many areas, we have social marketing, video marketing, mobile marketing, promotional marketing, traditional marketing, and new media marketing. There are of course the most obvious divisions between whom you market to, Business to Business, referred to as B2B, and then the Business to Customer, referred to as B2C.

Again, a recommendation to get started on an overall business plan is to pick up the software, *Marketing Plan Pro*. This software will walk you through many of the questions to at least start creating a marketing plan. But this is only a beginning. There are so many different areas of marketing, that one must find 'experts' in these areas that are willing to work with you in developing an action oriented marketing plan, based on your business plan.

There is a book, which again, I got with the software, but it is worth reading if you want a good place to start, for understanding and implementing a successful marketing plan.

The book is called, '_On Target: The Book on Marketing Plans_' and one of the authors once again is, Tim Berry.

This book also outlines many of the areas you must focus on, to successfully implement a marketing plan. But you also should have a marketing plan for nearly every product or service that you sell. You need to understand each product/service inside and out, and a marketing plan will help you do that.

I cannot stress how important it is to consult with marketing experts, if you are not one. Even experts in certain areas of marketing get someone to consult with them on other areas of marketing which they are not experts. Marketing these days covers a lot of ground, do not do yourself a disservice and neglect any part of it. Have I stressed it enough yet??

Step 5: Use Proper Advertising Plan(s).

Like your marketing plan, this step is placed here, not because it must be completed before you do the following 7 steps; but knowing and understanding each of the following steps will complete it. The rest of the steps are where you will be answering the questions needed to create, if not one, but potentially several, comprehensive advertising plans.

Your advertising plan is perhaps one of the most expensive, most exciting, most prone to waste and critical components of your entire marketing plan. (*This is most likely the first place Praecontitis will affect you.*) Yes, your advertising plan is a part of your marketing plan, just like your marketing plan is a part of your business plan. But only a small part, which is why there are three separate plans.[1]

Throughout the course of your business you will create, update or use more advertising plans, than any other type of plan you have. Advertising plans are the tactical action portions of your strategic action oriented marketing plan. They are generally more short term, more focused, and they typically need to be more flexible in their design. You may often hear these referred to as 'Campaigns'. You might have many campaigns going on at once, surrounding one single product or service.

Of course that means every one of your campaigns or advertising plans, will be a part of your strategic marketing plan. If you have a strong action oriented marketing plan, which was created properly, then you will be able to create many advertising plans that may be successful.

Advertising is full of testing, testing, and oh yeah, did I say testing. Until you find that magic formula, everything is a test. Even after you find that perfect campaign that converts better than all the rest, you will still be testing and finding ways to tweak it a little more, or finding new campaigns to test against your control. In copywriting you refer to the piece that is proven and used over and over again, as the control.

Just like in science, even if a new campaign works better and beats your control, you still must repeat the process. If you can't repeat the results over and over again, then the new campaign does not replace your old control. When you are creating an advertising plan, you will draw from the research you did in the marketing planning stage.

Does your advertising plan, meet the goals of your overall marketing plan? Does it fit your current budget? Does it use the most appropriate mediums for your business?

It's time to make a point, and some might consider it a little controversial. But it is somewhat of a pet peeve of mine when people confuse marketing and advertising. I will explain why knowing the difference is important in a minute.

You must realize and understand that not only is there is a distinct difference between a business plan, a marketing plan, and an advertising plan, but marketing is also NOT the same thing as advertising, please don't confuse the two. Advertising is merely a part of everything included within marketing.

Many people presume and often intermix the words, marketing and advertising, when they are not the same, they just have a very strong relationship, but that does not mean they are the same thing, nor should they be treated as the same thing.

Marketing is the entire process from the beginning of a product or services life, until that product or service no longer exists. Marketing starts the moment a product or service is conceived in the mind of a person. It includes the rigorous hours of research, gathering data, and discovering whether a market even exists for the product or service. It includes planning different strategies for product placement, in the marketing mix, as well as, within the general market place.

Advertising is a large piece of the overall marketing plan; it is the sexy part of marketing, as one of my professors in college used to say. Advertising is the most visible portion of marketing; it is the part that business owners often believe gets the most results, it is the flashy part of the marketing plan, and often a large piece of the action portion. Since it is mistakenly seen as the primary results oriented part of marketing, it is not a wonder that everyone wants to be most involved with this part.

Sales in all its forms are a rather large part of what makes up this thing we refer to as advertising.

Why is this important?

Let's first start by taking the dictionary definitions of both.

- Marketing is *"The action or business of promoting and selling products or services, including market research and advertising."*

- Advertising is: *"The activity or profession of producing advertisements for commercial products or services."*

Note that advertising is mentioned as a part of marketing. But marketing is not mentioned at all in the definition of advertising.

Advertising is a channel, which is used by marketers to promote a product/service they are selling. Sales is an extension to Advertising. It is also a channel that marketers use to promote and sell a product. But marketing is the entire process.

Another definition of marketing which I like, comes from the '*On Target*' Book. It says:
"Marketing - The set of planned activities designed to positively influence the perceptions and purchase choices of individuals and organizations."

I like this definition because it emphasizes how marketing is a set of *planned* activities. Marketing covers all aspects of advertising and sales, and distribution, and everything else you can think of to promote, sell or learn more about a product/service.

Marketing is more than just placing some ads or selling to people. A marketer must fully understand what is being sold, why it is being sold, how it is being sold, and more importantly whom it is being sold to.

Marketers set the groundwork for amazing advertising. The better the marketing, the better the advertising has the potential to be. If the advertiser does not understand the market they are trying to sell to and they do not have a clear direction, then it is likely that a business will experience, Praeconititus. Remember this is where the Praeconititus bug is most likely to hit the hardest.

Some marketers have the potential to be great sales people, especially if they understand the advertising portion of the plan better than anything else. Someone with a strong advertising background also has the potential to be very good at sales, as sales and advertising are very closely related activities. In both cases as long as they happen to know when to shut up, they will probably do well.

From personal experience, I can say that I have talked customers out of more sales than I care to admit. The reason being, I believed that like me, the person needed to know EVERYTHING about what they were buying. I'm a marketer pure and simple and it is my job to know everything I can about the product and whom I am selling it to. I need to be able to see inside my customer's heads and predict what is best. Or at least test out my ideas.

But in sales, I often forgot the magic of emotion and the idea that if the question does not come up, then it is probably not a concern that needs to be dealt with. I, in my infinite wisdom, would create concerns that people never had, and overthink the situation and this would make people hesitant, which equated to wanting to wait and not buy what I was selling.

My point is whatever you do, do not mistake that these are two completely separate activities. If you are a salesman, you may want to work very closely with a marketer to develop your marketing plan, and help you develop more leads and other information to help you sell better. If you are a marketer, but love sales, then you may need to outsource many of the marketing activities, so you can focus more on the advertising and sales aspect of your business. Of course if you happen to be a marketer, but maybe not a salesmen, either take the time to learn sales, or outsource it.

(Note the Glossary at the end of this book that details the easiest ways to understand the primary differences between each of the different types of plans, in order to more effectively use them in your business.[1])

Center of Influence Marketing

Normal advertising is a complete waste of money. Why? Because normal advertising will get you normal results. You don't become an industry leader or a dominant presence by doing things the "normal" way.

Most small businesses advertise in the Yellow Pages. However, I think you're going to find Yellow Page advertising is going to become weaker and weaker, because more people now use the Internet to find their information.

Besides, almost all Yellow Page ads look the same. Hmmmm... could it be because they're all designed by the same person? Of course, this means that everybody's ad is (by definition) "normal".

Newspaper advertising is also falling. But let's look at it – again almost all the ads look the same. Could it be because they are all designed by the same person? Hmmm... If everything looks normal, everybody gets normal results.

Finally, consider this – you're advertising in the same place as your competitors. That's kind of dumb, isn't it? I'd rather advertise in a vacuum, where I'm the only choice.

You have to think outside the box. I fashion myself as a collector of good ideas. I look for those different ways of advertising that don't get normal results... but extraordinary results.

What I'm about to show you is going to give you a far greater return than normal advertising ever will. It will also dramatically enhance the relationship you have with your fellow business owners and finally it'll just make others think you're some sort of genius because of your innovation.

I'm talking about center of influence marketing. Here's the premise – instead of going out and hunting down your ideal prospects, what would happen if you already went to where a bunch of them hang out, and just put your sign up in front of them?

You're going to where they already are, instead of picking them up "one by one" in the newspaper, on the television, or in the Yellow Pages.

Okay, so here's what you're going to do – you're going to come up with a bunch of different places where your ideal customers frequent in large numbers. Then you're going to construct an offer that will allow you to siphon those ideal customers off into your own sales funnel. And, it's only going to cost you a small "toll booth" fee to do this, which you will only pay out of a portion of the profits you're generating.

Let's take a second to talk about targeted marketing. Say you and I both owned a pizza place. I would only need one competitive advantage, and I could destroy you and win every single customer. I'd give you all other advantages, because, when totaled, they still wouldn't give you a chance.

Yes, I would give you the best ingredients. I'd give you the best employees. I'd give you the best location. I'd give you the coolest store layout. I'd only ask for one thing...

I'd only ask that all my customers are dying of hunger!

When someone is hungry, they don't care what your store looks like. They don't care if you have good service. They don't care if the food even tastes good. They are just so hungry that they'll practically pay anything and eat anything to quell that hunger.

What targeted marketing does is isolates and focuses your efforts on singling out those who are "hungriest" for whatever you offer.

Let me make it real to you. Let's say you're in the retail flooring business. Okay, now people who buy flooring... what else do they tend to need that complements that?

Well, a lot of people who need flooring also need paint. What would happen if you had a majority of the paint stores sending the customers who needed flooring your way?

If I wanted to market to small businesses to offer my marketing consultation services, where would I go? Well, I might start with local accountants, because they help a lot of business owners with their taxes.

I might also go to the heads of trade associations that small business owners would be a member of (like the chambers of commerce, for example), and volunteer for free to give a speech where I'd share my expertise on how to get more customers.

I may also go to attorneys that help people form corporations, and attorneys who specialize in helping small businesses.

See what I'm doing here? I'm finding a complementary, non-competitive business entity that already attracts the "hungry" customers that I'm in search of. Instead of having to find those customers myself, I'm leveraging their efforts.

Now, here's how to NOT make this work. Go up to one of these centers of influence and say, "Hey, why don't you tell your customers to come to me when they need X." This is completely ridiculous.

You have to make it make sense for them to refer others to you before they will. What's an easy way to do this? Why not say, "Hey, I know from time to time you have customers that also need my services. So how do you feel about this? Every time you send someone over my way, and they become my customer, I give you X% of the sale?"

Warning – in some industries, it's illegal to do this. And since I'm no lawyer, check the laws first to make sure that you can legally do this. I'm just giving you one example here. There are other ways you can reward them.

For example, send customers to *them* in return. It could be as simple as making a stack of fliers up to put in their business, and they do likewise to distribute at your business. Now it's a "referral revolving door" and more importantly... it's a win-win situation.

Here's how you can make it work for you. First, pull out the Yellow Pages. Go through them, and each time you find a category that would be complementary to your business, write it down.

Get 5-10 different complementary "industries", and then pick the top 3 businesses in each of those industries. Now you have a list of 15-30 businesses to approach.

Second, create your irresistible offer for these business-es. If you can give them a cash incentive for a referral, then consider that as your offer. Or come up with something equally enticing that answers their number one question -- "What's in it for me?"

Another thing you can do here is to give a special offer just for *their* customers. It could be a discount, or something extra they get for free that you would normally charge for. This way, the "What's in it for me?" is that their customers will like them more, because it looks like the owner went to bat and negotiated a special deal just for them.

How many businesses could you do this with? Well, as many as you would like. This can take care of the new customer acquisition end of things, especially when you combine it with referral marketing.

Think about it – you could easily get ten businesses that were complementary to you to promote for you for some sort of incentive.

For some, it might just be that you put up some fliers at the counter, with a special "freebie" just for their customers. For other businesses, it might be a customer exchange. You send customers their way if they send customers your way. For others still, it might work to downright pay them a cut of the sales.

In any case, realize the importance behind this – most of the cost for customer acquisition will only be paid after the customer is acquired. You pay a percentage of the sale – after the sale is made. You get referrals because you refer.

This truly takes the risk out of advertising, because you'll only pay for it if it works. Not a bad deal!

Step 6: Integrate Online Marketing Tactics.

If you have a brick and mortar business and you do not have a website of your own, then the first question is why not? Then next we would say, shame on you for not having one yet, but what can we do to fix it?

For most businesses, regardless of product or service offered, not having a website is a recipe for disaster. For many businesses, especially those that are only 'online businesses', this step could and probably should be the most important step. For these businesses, each of the other steps in the 12 step process will focus on the different stages of *integrating* all your *online marketing* activities.

Don't be fooled by seeing that this is only one step of twelve (12), because the importance of the online portion of your plan cannot be overstated in today's market. But there is no cookie cutter solution or one size fits all plan and like most of the steps in the Relationship Marketing Model, it will take time, effort and planning to effectively Integrate all of your Online Marketing Tactics.

(Note: *Even if your business is primarily based online, all steps in the Relationship Marketing Model are still important.*)

Answer these questions. Do you have a website? What is the purpose or goal of your website? Can your customers effectively find you online?

Once on your website, is it easily navigable and does it meet the goals you have set for having it? Are you implementing quality SEO practices?

Do you have an article marketing campaign? What information are you providing to your customers for free? How often do you update your website?

Does your advertising plan include using your website? Is your website inline with the overall goals of your business and marketing plans? Is your online presence an effective part of your advertising strategy?

How integrated is your social media plans, into your marketing plans? Do you employ video marketing?

Are you doing mobile marketing? Do you have a blog that you update regularly?

5 Proven Internet Strategies to Explode Your Local Sales

1 Video Marketing

Would you believe that there are over 26 BILLION videos viewed per month in the United States alone? What's more, YouTube is the #2 search engine on the Internet, which means that <u>right now</u> somebody is likely searching for your services online in the form of a video.

Imagine if you had the budget to run infomercials 24 hours a day, 7 days a week…you'd dominate your market! That's the power of video marketing. Let me show you how this is possible on a shoestring (even in a terrible economy!), and be able to engender more trust and respect with your customers than ever before.

#2 Lead-Capture and Follow-up Campaigns

Did you know that an even GREAT webpage will only convert 5% of its visitors into a purchase? It's absolutely true, and this means that 19 out of 20 visitors to your website are destined to surf away into the ether…and likely find your competitor's website instead.

However the AVERAGE page that offers consumers <u>free information</u> in exchange for their contact info gets 35-40% conversion.

Imagine being able to instantly increase your return on leads 7-FOLD, and do it with push button automation. This is possible, and I or another Internet marketing professional can show you how.

3 Local Search Visibility

Did you know that 30% of all searches online include a city or local term (like "Portland Plumbing Contractors")?

This means that every search for every term will have the local companies that have figured out how to get listed in all of the local directories.

It goes without saying that your customers can't hire you if they can't find you online. I or another expert 12 step consultant can make sure that your local business is **found** on Google...for all of the keywords that you need to rank for so that your neighbors can find you online.

4 Social Media Marketing

With over 1 Billion members (and counting), Facebook is a giant that cannot be ignored. Social networks have changed the way people research and make buying decisions. But Facebook is not the only social network; there are dozens of them. Which ones are right for you?

When leveraged in your favor you'll have the opportunity to build more trust, respect, and credibility than ever before.

Imagine being able to have feedback on how to improve your business, and sell more on a daily basis. Imagine being able to turn every customer into a potential raving fan who will advertise for you. An Internet marketing professional, like myself, can make it happen, and you can secure my services exclusively in your local market.

5 Blog Marketing

Did you know that 77% of all Internet users follow one or more blogs? If you're not capitalizing on the growing community, you're missing out on huge business.

Bloggers are passionate about sharing, and if you have one as a client and can turn them into a raving fan, they can propel your business to new heights.

Let me help you create and manage your video blog, all with push-button simplicity so you can leverage this influence-engine giant for your benefit…and increase your bottom line year after year.

Step 7: Human Resources - Employee Acquisition.

Develop programs around your Employees, future potential employees or even the benefits you want for yourself. Yes, Human Resources are a vital, but often overlooked part of a successful marketing plan.

The first step in the HR process is Employee Acquisition. You must first attract the employees or contractors that will best fit your business.

How do you know if they fit your business?

One way to know is having a thorough interview process. As part of that process, have personality, interest, and maybe even skills based testing to find out how your prospective employees will best fit into your organization. If you are planning to fit a contractor into a critical role, it is often very valuable to do the same thing. The more you can learn about anyone that you plan to work with, whether internally or externally, the better it will be for your business in the long run.

In reality, the better it will also be for anyone you work with too. You will find that their level of happiness, the level of loyalty, and the level of overall production will increase quite dramatically, but most of all everyone in your business, including you will have much lower levels of overall frustration. If sanity is not enough to get you to explore using tests, then I really don't know what is.

If you are a start-up or have only been in business for a few years, then your number one employee is yourself. Yes, until you have built your business to a point that you no longer have to work everyday, you must remember that you are your most important employee and you must reward yourself, just as you would any other employee. You are going to want to think about your own benefits for yourself and your family.

Ask yourself, what is your ROI on your benefits? Other than a decent wage, what other benefits or incentives are you offering prospective employees? Do you offer hiring bonuses, as a standard way 0f attracting new employees?

Maybe you don't plan to have employees at all; maybe you plan to use contractors to outsource everything. If this is the case, how and where do you find contractors? What incentives will you offer to them, if any?

As part of the planning process you need to look very carefully at your business and decide whether you want to use employees or contractors or both. You must weigh the pros and cons of each option. It is important to think both short and long-term. You may decide as part of your business plan that you do not want to grow your business very big. So the number of employees you need may be very small. Or that you wont have any employees and instead will just have a few contractors.

Whatever you decide, it is important that your working business plan reflect your ideas and that your overall marketing plan, has an action item that reflects where, how, when, and even if you will have employees or contractors.

Step 8: Human Resources - Employee Retention.

Employee Retention is the second half of the HR process, but a very, very important part. If you don't plan this portion of your marketing plan effectively, you will waste a significant amount of money constantly hiring new employees to fill the vacancies.

How you treat your employees will be a direct reflection on how your customers are treated. Also, it is important to remember that wages and salaries are only one factor in retaining employees and it often isn't even a leading factor.

To illustrate this point, several years ago, I had a friend who was having a difficult time financially. He and his wife had no jobs and needed some sort of an income, or they were going to be left with nothing. It just so happens, we were thinking about hiring a receptionist for our office that would not only answer calls and set appointments but also do some outbound calling and other light computer work. We offered her the job.

To make a long story short, she was a hard worker whenever someone was breathing down her neck and upset with her. But as soon as you would give her praise at a job well done, she would slack off and quit working. Money had nothing to do with her motivation to work. She was there because she had to be, but she also was very negatively motivated.

It began to be very draining for us to constantly either micro-manage her every move, which the reason we hired her was to free us up to do more profitable tasks, or we were forced to constantly get upset with her about the quality of her work or not finishing something on time.

We tested our theory out and her productivity levels would more than double any time someone questioned her or in any way got upset with the quality of her work. Whenever we praised her for a job well done, because when she worked she did fabulous work, her level of work dropped to almost nothing.

After a short time, we finally had to let her go. Needless to say it was an expensive and valuable lesson in employee motivation. It is important to know and understand what motivates your employees to work. Know what it is about the work you are providing that attracts them to it.

What are you going to do to reward your employees and create an atmosphere of loyalty?

As you may already know, loyalty in the workplace is virtually non-existent. On average people change jobs once every 5 years, but it does not have to be this way. Of course you are not going to keep everyone, but if you have planned effectively, and you are addressing the needs of those that work for you, then you may find that loyalty to your workplace has a much higher average.

Some questions to ask yourself are what training do you offer? Are you providing a way for those that work for you to continue to grow professionally? Do you offer any sort of educational benefits? If so, what are the conditions that you place on receiving those benefits?

Do you have an employee incentive program? I don't mean, do you offer them cash rewards and bonuses, although it may be helpful to do that too, depending on the position and their personality. I am referring to what other outside incentives do you offer? Is there an opportunity to earn vacations, awards, or anything that is going to be memorable to those that work for you?

Before we go any further, there is a question that may have crossed your mind. Why is there a section about Employee Acquisition and Retention, before anything about customers?

Are Employees More Important Than Customers?

Simple answer... YES! Most definitely. Even if you are the only employee, you must first take care of yourself or soon you will not have a business. Never forget, how you treat your employees has a direct result on how THEY treat your customers.

If you are a sole proprietor and for whatever reason you never plan to have employees, then you still must first take care of yourself and all parts of your business, or as already mentioned there will be no business. In this case, it means you create a plan for your family and yourself.

It's OK to be a little selfish towards your business when planning certain parts of your marketing strategy.

Step 9: Customer Acquisition.

Without customers you don't have a business. Customers are the reason you are in business. Other than your employees, Customers are the most valuable asset your business has, they are more valuable than any building, piece of equipment, or intellectual property.

In order to acquire customers, you must first know and understand the need you fill with your products and services and also identify or better clarify your target market. Oh, wait a minute, does this vaguely sound like the job of marketing? Research, research, research.

You must create an ideal customer. Give them a name, job, perhaps a family if that is part of your ideal customer. Design a fictitious person and describe every part of who and what makes that person who they are, don't leave any details out. Tell a story about your customers.

Bob is 35 years old married with two kids, both under the age of 10. He drives a Mercedes and works at a local technology firm, etc., etc.

In the beginning, this is the best way to truly understand your customer. Then comes the fun part, or some might say the hard part. The testing. Test, test, and test some more and then be patient, very, very patient. Make sure your assumptions were correct. Marketing is a lot of testing, because you deal with people and people can change like the weather. A change in the economy, a change in the political climate, a change in technology, innovation, or nearly anything else, can cause things to change. Be prepared for the one constant that you can count on, change and lots of it.

Are you starting to see why updating your marketing plan, and even your business plan, is important yet? I hope you understand by now that marketing is a process that never ends. It is a living, breathing part of your business, and you cannot neglect it for one second. Whether your customer is another business, the government, or everyday consumers, they are the reason your business exists. Without them, you have no business, so treat them as if your life depends on it, because the life of your business truly does.

The *Right* Way to Place Print or Digital Ads

Have you noticed that 95% of Yellow Page ads look the same? There's a problem with going with the "norm" -- you get normal results.

With your business and livelihood on the line, I hope you're not content with average results, especially when extraordinary results are so easy to get with Yellow Pages or any other type of Print Ads. You only need to do a few simple things.

Throughout this section we will talk about the Yellow Pages quite a bit. Even though the Yellow Pages are dying, for some businesses it still makes sense. There are still those people out there that either don't have a computer or smartphone, (ah, blasphemy!), or rarely use them, or simply do not know how to use them yet.

Depending on your demographics, it might still be a good idea to use Yellow Pages, at least for a little while longer anyway. But also note that these techniques are not exclusive to placing Yellow Page ads. They are transferable to many other types of print and online ads, so pay attention, you might actually learn something.

The first thing you have to understand is what people are looking for when they open up the yellow pages. Some people are looking for SPECIFIC contact information. They already have a service provider in mind. It's hard to get those people. *(However, it is important to make that contact information easy to find and access. We'll talk about this a little more later.)*

But the good news is when most people open up the Yellow Pages; they are looking for information *to help them find the best business to contact* that will give them the solution they desire.

Here's what most consumers want: They want a good deal, they want to go with someone who is able to understand their needs and lead them to the best solution, and they want to deal with as little headaches, delays and customer service problems as possible.

Now, flip open your yellow pages and see if any of the ads address those points, and you'll find hardly any do so adequately.

Good. That will make it much easier for you.

I'm going to show you how to create a simple yellow page ad that will make people believe that if they contact you or go into your store that they are going to get the best solution for their dollars, and it's going to be easy and convenient to deal with you, and that you're the best choice for all of their options.

If you can pull that off, you're going to get the lion's share of Yellow Page customers in your industry.

The Most Important Part of Your Ad

The world's best ad is no better than the world's worst ad if no one sees it. So the first job your Yellow Page ad must do is get the attention of the people who are best matched to take advantage of the services and products that you offer.

The easiest way to do that is with a good attention-getting headline.

To understand what a good headline looks like, first let's look at some bad headlines. I went through my own local Yellow Pages, and found these headlines:

"The Blind Factory"

"Cyclists Serving Cyclists"

"Wet Basement or Crawl Space"

"Quality Construction"

"Professional Muffler, Inc."

"Old Fashioned Values, Including Our Own People Doing the Work"

These are all terrible headlines, and I bet you can find many of the same ones in your local Yellow Pages. First, almost all of them talk about the service provider, and not the person who is looking at the ad. Talk about selfish and self-centered!

Second, none of them promise any benefit to the person... none of them get the person reading excited... and most are nothing more than the name of the company.

Your headline is the most important part of your yellow page ad so you need to do better. Ideally, you want a headline that promises a benefit to the reader, and is written to grab the attention of a certain large segment of the population who is best matched for the goods and services you provide.

Let's look at the first one -- "The Blind Factory". How could this one be improved? Here is a good headline that I have found gets great results... "The 6 Mistakes Most People Make When They Purchase Blinds For Their Home..."

Or... "Warning: Don't Buy Any Blinds Until You Read This..." Or Even "How to Get the Best Blinds For Your Home in 48 Hours Or Less, Guaranteed!"

Notice the difference with these headlines? First, they focus on the consumer. Second, they promise a huge benefit. Third, they call out a certain portion of the general population – in this case, people who are looking to purchase blinds, who want to get a good deal, want ease of service, or want to make sure they don't commit a mistake when buying blinds. Hm, sound familiar?

Once you have a good headline, the ad practically writes itself. For example, let's return to the headline: "The 6 Mistakes People Make When They Purchase Blinds for Their Home". You would then come up with 6 mistakes that you find people tend to make if they don't have an expert to help them select their product. And then, after you introduce each mistake, explain how that mistake can be avoided if they come into your store.

Remember, people who open up the Yellow Page ads are generally looking for *information to help them make the best decision* on whom to buy from. So typically the person who provides the most information wins... and it helps if that information is all beneficial to the reader.

But if you look at the typical Yellow Page ad, it has 50 words or less, and is usually filled with puffery. For example, I always see "The customer comes first". And I always say – prove it!

Which leads us to the second biggest point about writing effective Yellow Pages ads: making powerful, unique claims to demonstrate that you're better than any other solution that's available in the Yellow Pages or whatever directory you are listed in.

So how can you make a unique claim that demonstrates that "the customer comes first"?

Here's a technique that's been used to great effect. The first thing you do is contact some of your past satisfied customers. Then, you ask them to write a quick one-paragraph testimonial about what they liked most about dealing with you. (*It's easy to do this with the right strategy*).

Then, you put all those testimonials on a website. Now, in your ad you can say, "You can even read what 117 satisfied customers had to say about our great products at..." and then put the website address in there.

Now, most people looking at the ad WON'T go to the page and read it. But it will have the effect of demonstrating to them that not only does the customer come first, but also that you have 117 of your own customers who say that you DO put them first. You'll be the only ad in your category that can claim that, so in people's minds you'll be the preferred source if customer service is their main priority.

At any rate, your ad should contain at least one dramatic example of proof to validate your claims. It's best if you have specific numbers or facts to verify it, testimonials to show and other powerful ways to demonstrate that you offer great service and goods.

For example, you can do much better than merely stating something like "In business since 1972!" My first reaction when I see this statement is "So what?"

The fact is, I know a lot of bad companies that have stayed in business for decades. Instead, you can say, "We've successfully helped over 10,678 clients in [city name] find the right blinds for their home."

So first come up with a powerful headline. Then, expand on that headline in your ad, and also throw in at least one dramatic example of proof to validate your claims.

Now you only have to do one final thing.

Have an Offer And a "Call To Action"

Every single ad you write should have an offer and a call-to-action to accept that offer. A call to action means that you tell them exactly what they should do after reading the ad.

Let me start with the best call to action, although it's also the most complicated one to set up.

What you ideally want is a continuing relationship with people who are interested in doing business with you, so if they are hesitant initially, further communication can get them in the door.

The best way to do that is to offer something free to the user if they contact you. Here's a simple way to do that. Let's go back to the Blinds example.

The first thing you'd want to do is sit down and write a little 6-8 page report on "How to Pick The Most Beautiful Blinds For Your Home On A Shoe-string Budget" or something like that.

Then just give them the best tips for getting the most value from their purchase.

What you're going to want to do next is take that report (*written on a computer*) and export it as a PDF (*you can do this for free with OpenOffice, which you can download on the internet*).

Then, you're going to want to set up an "autoresponder" account at aweber.com, getresponse.com, constantcontact.com or a number of other providers. This allows you to have people sign up for an email list, so you can send them emails in the future. Depending on the strategy that you and an expert at online marketing may come up with there are other options as well, but the most important point, is you need a way to collect their data and build your own list. This is key, don't forget this.

Then, if they sign up for your list, they will automatically get delivered your free digital report on "How to Pick The Most Beautiful Blinds For Your Home On A Shoe-string Budget." Not only that, you can use your autoresponder to send a few follow up messages automatically at certain intervals to anyone who signs up. This is one reason you need a list.

Then in your Yellow Page or other ad you say, "If you'd like to get our free report on "How to Pick The Most Beautiful Blinds For Your Home On A Shoe-string Budget", then just go to www.yourwebsiteaddress.com". This drives them to a page that explains that in order to get the report they just have to enter in their name and email into the form. (*Don't worry the form will be created automatically for you, with most legitimate auto-responder services.*)

Of course, in the report you're going to want to put your contact information so if they read it they can easily contact you and become your customer.

This is by far the best strategy but also the most complex. A simple strategy is to make a "Yellow Page ad only" offer. In this case you say, "If you call us today to schedule an appointment, and mention that you are calling because of the Yellow Page ad, we'll give a 10% off Yellow Page 'special deal".

Another simple strategy to use is SMS messaging. Get either an 'SMS Shortcode' or a service that allows you to capture information through an SMS phone number. Then you can say, just text your name and email to: xxx-xxx-xxxx or something like that.

But why would you want to use SMS messaging in your marketing?

Let's take a quick second to explore why using SMS Marketing is beneficial to your business. Here are a few statistics about SMS:

- There are 7.2 billion mobile subscribers (*that's more than 100 percent of the world population*). (*October 2014*)

- SMS is still king of mobile messaging with more than 6.1 trillion messages sent in 2010. Despite the popularity of mobile email, IM and MMS, SMS is predicted to exceed 10 trillion in 2013.
- According to consumer research by The MMA and Lightspeed Research (October 2010), in UK, France and Germany, 45 percent of consumers (especially younger people) noticed mobile advertising and of these, 29 percent responded to it. Of those that responded to the ads, in Germany 49 percent, UK 47 percent, and in France 22 percent went on to make purchases.
- The most effective form of ads was opt-in SMS in the UK (40 percent said they were more likely to respond to these) and in France (21 percent); while in Germany it was mobile Web ads (27 percent). Time sensitive special offers or discounts were most likely to lead to purchase.
- Four out of five teens carry a wireless device, and the majority (57%) views their cell phone as the key to their social life.

With a 98% open rate for text messages, what form of marketing would be a more efficient use of your marketing dollars? Oh, and when we say dollars, we actually mean cents. It's really that affordable.

So other than cost, what other reason might you use SMS or some form of mobile marketing in your ad?

The reason is simple, to build a list.

Remember we mentioned a list earlier and how you could send them a free report and then a series of autoresponder messages. By using the right SMS service, you are doing two things at once.

You are sending the free digital report on "How to Pick The Most Beautiful Blinds For Your Home On A Shoe-String Budget." and you are not only building your list for Email, but you are building a Mobile list as well. Since we know that Mobile marketing is powerful, why not combine it with email; this strategy will undoubtedly dramatically increase the open rates of your email messages.

The importance of building sales funnels and lists for any business cannot be over stated. This is how you get your message in front of a much more targeted audience, for a lot less money.

In any case, the point of adding a call to action that is of immediate and long-term value is that you're enticing them to respond to your ad.

If you do all of the things in this chapter, then you're going to have an ad that is dramatically different than everyone else's which will allow you to get dramatically better results!

Step 10: Customer Retention.

Ever notice how telecommunication companies seem to spend a huge amount of their time, effort and money on finding new customers? But then once you become a customer, they seem to forget who you are?

If you happen to live in an area, where you have an actual choice in these services, ask yourself how many times in the last 10 or 20 years you have switched providers. Why did you switch? I bet it had a lot to do with a competing company having a great offer that sounded really good to you.

Now ask yourself this question. Ever been a customer of a telecom company and see a pretty great offer advertised and wonder, why can't I get that?   Maybe you were like me and you actually called in and asked if you qualified and got a pretty long-winded answer at why you did not. The answer may have gone something like this:

> "We can't offer that too you, because you are a current customer and you already have a fantastic deal. We are a business so we have to make our money someplace." My first thought, "Yeah right! Are you kidding me?"

Then if you are anything like me you thought, why don't you ever have offers for your current customers? Or even have better customer only offers that reward customers for loyalty. Perhaps an upgrade on some service for free, like HBO or Starz or a bigger package, after you have been a customer for a year or 18 months. Why not allow customers to get special offers?

Why don't these huge companies that have millions of dollars, spend more money and time on their current customers, instead of spending all the money they do on acquiring new ones, only to lose their current ones, to the competitors next best 'deal of the month'?

It doesn't make a lot of sense does it? In the next two chapters, we'll be talking more about this phenomenon.

Here is a list of questions you should be answering in this part of your overall planning process.

- How will you keep your customers loyal to your products and services? Note Mistake #1, in the Chapter Don't Leave Money on the Table.
- How do you keep your customers from going to your competition instead of you or should you even try?
- Are there strategic partnerships that can benefit your business and your customers? If so, how do you identify them?
- Other than the product or service itself and meeting the basic expectations the consumer already has, what are you doing extra for your customers?
- Do you have a referral program?
- Are you using promotionals, to effectively help your customers remember you? If you are, are your promotionals somehow different or more useful than those of your competitors?
- Why should your customers remember you and your business? Have you given them a reason to do so?

How to Find Customers for Life

Imagine that there was a huge amount of oil buried right outside in your backyard. We're talking millions of dollars worth.

Would that make you rich? Not if you didn't know about it! You could live your whole life sitting on "liquid gold" and be none the wiser.

However, if I came up to you and told you about it, and showed you beyond a shadow of doubt that there was oil and you drilled for it. Then you'd be filthy rich.

In most small business, there DOES exist a situation that is similar to the oil well example above. Most small business owners are sitting on a potential fortune and they don't even realize it.

In this chapter I'm going to share with you perhaps the single most effective strategy for mining the "hidden gold" that is likely to exist in your business.

The Forgotten "Rule" Of An Obscure Italian Economist

In 1906 a man by the name of Vilfredo Pareto discovered something unusual about the Italian economy – 80% of the wealth was controlled by 20% of the population.

Was this just an anomaly? Turns out it wasn't. In Britain he found the same thing to be true and found it to be true in pretty much all economies. But what's interesting is that this unequal distribution exists outside of economies as well. For example, studies have shown in general that:

80% of traffic accidents are committed by 20% of drivers

80% of crimes are committed by 20% of the population

80% of a company's output comes from 20% of its employees, and most importantly of all...

80% of your profits come from only 20% of your customers!

This is almost always true. So what's that mean for you?

Simple: if you can isolate who those "20 percenters" are, and then come up with a marketing plan that will attract more customers like those "20 percenters" and also create additional products, services and offers for your "20 percenters" then...

You should be able to, very easily, add 20% to your bottom-line profits within the next 90 days.

Where To Start

In an ideal situation, you've kept track of your past customers purchases, so you can access their records. What you want to do is go through and first isolate customers who have spent the *most* money with you.

Now, that doesn't necessarily mean that they are your most profitable customers. They are just your highest grossing customers. Unfortunately, gross does not always mean more profitable! However, it's a good place to start.

After you find your highest grossing customers, then analyze your profit margin on those customers, to narrow it down even more. To make it easy for you, come up with your 50 "highest grossing customers", and out of those 50, arrange them in order of *most profitable*, in terms of percentages.

Now take your 20 "Most profitable" customers, and analyze them. What we are looking for are demographics and psychographics.

Demographics are things such as:

- Size of Household

- Annual Income Earned

- Age

- Gender

- Geographical Location

Psychographics are:

- What clubs they belong to

- What their hobbies and interests are

- Their Values

- Their Opinions

- Lifestyle & other behavior attributes

In other words, you are trying to isolate their "culture" if you will.

How can this be helpful to you? Well, let's say you analyze your results and find out that your most profitable customers are typically:

White, aged 45-50, have 2-3 children, are married, live on the northeast side of town, make between $75,000 to $100,000 a year, are active in the community, especially with charitable events, typically play a lot of golf and/or tennis, are conservative republicans, and often take 2-3 vacations a year.

That's some valuable information! (Sidebar: *Remember the story we talked about previously? This is an example of a story you need to know about your customers. Make your customers come alive and then create marketing that talks to those people. Know your market.*) For starters, did you know you could rent a list in your area with those "selects" (*select is just a fancy term for different attributes*)?

Yes, for a fee you could get a list of all the people in your city that are between 45-50, living in a certain zip code, making an annual income of $75,000 to $100,000 a year. And that's just a few of the "selects" you can specify. You can even go deeper if you wish.

These are the type of prospects you want to spend your money marketing to! While past results do not necessarily guarantee future behavior, they are about as good an indicator to go by as any. The point is, if that type of customer was profitable to you in the past, it stands to reason similar people who fit that description will also be extremely profitable for you NOW.

Then what do you do? The best thing is to create a direct mail campaign and send a letter to each name on the list you rented making them a special offer.

You want to write an advertisement that is personable, explains the benefits of your services, and makes a special "introductory offer" to get them into your place of business.

Even better is if, in those advertisements, you talk about things like golf and tennis, taking vacations, saying things that conservative republicans are known to agree with, and talk about charitable events. This helps build rapport with the prospect. You just have to tie those things to your sales message and offer it in some creative way.

And that's just one simple example of how to make the "80/20" rule work in your favor.

Here's an even better example: Look into your customer records of your most profitable customers and ask yourself, "What services and goods can I offer them that they don't currently have, but would be complementary to purchases they've made in the past?"

If someone is a very profitable customer to you, it usually means that they like doing business with you, need a lot of what you have to offer, trust you, and often think of you as the "go-to" solution for problems related to your area of service and expertise.

So if you have a good recommendation that could help bring them value to their life, and is a perfect fit for something you've offered them in the past, you're likely to meet with success.

Here's how you can maximize your efforts. Start with your top 20 customers. What you want to do is write a PERSONAL letter to each of them. Start with talking about how you were analyzing your past records and noticed that they have been a very good customer, and that you value their business. Then say you also noticed something that may be a benefit, and since they've been a good customer you're going to give them a special deal next time they come into the store and purchase something from you. Give them specific examples, such as...

"I noticed you purchased X from us. Well a new product we just got rights to complements X perfectly, so if you come in within the next 2 weeks I can give you a special deal of 40% off the shelf price. This is just my way of saying thanks for being such a valuable customer."

Another strategy to consider is the referral strategy. Think about this: people typically hang around others who share their same values and beliefs. This is a perfect way to attract new customers who are likely to be just as profitable as your past "most profitable customers".

In this case, you'd send your best customers a letter, and let them know that you're making them a "valued customer special offer" if they recommend someone to your business, and you'll give their referrals a "preferred VIP discount" or "preferred VIP treatment", since they came from a highly valued source.

People love to refer when this is the case. It makes them look good in front of their friends, and a lot of people get value in that. It's also great for you, because word of mouth advertising is some of the best advertising there is. Also, if you can just get these referrals into the door and have them start a buying relationship with you, chances are they will continue to buy from you in the future. Thus you will get more than just a one-off purchase, you may get a customer for life with a high lifetime value.

Don't Leave Money on the Table!

Do you know the 3 Deadly Mistakes that almost all small businesses are making? If you don't, you are not alone. Most entrepreneurs simply have never considered the fact that by making these 3 small tweaks to their current business; they can increase sales by up to 20% within the next 100 days. It's absolutely true.

I know that some of these ideas will shock you...and in fact I hope they do. Why? Because my job is to help you take a fresh look at your own business, and evaluate the areas that can be improved *right now* in order to create more sales & improve your bottom line immediately.

Mistake #1: Going After New Customers

Yes, you read that right. New customers are the most expensive people in the world to find, attract into your place of business, and then convert into customers.

To help you understand this, let me demonstrate to you a powerful fact.

There are only 3 ways to increase your profits.

The first way is to increase your number of customers. If Bob has a lemonade stand and sells 100 cups a day to 100 people and makes $0.10 a cup for a total of $10 a day in profit... If Bob figures out a way to get 200 people to buy a cup he's just doubled his profits.

But that's not the only way Bob can double his profit. What if he figures out a way for his customers to purchase two cups of lemonade each? By doing so, he will be able to double his profits with the same number of customers.

And what if Bob were to offer something for his customers to purchase that is complimentary to the lemonade...such as a hot dog? Then, if a certain percentage *also* buys a hot dog when he sells them lemonade, he can double his sales.

So let's review: here are the only three ways that you will ever be able to grow your business and increase your profits:

- More customers

- Same customers purchase more stuff

- Same customers making more frequent purchases

Of the three, which is the most profitable? Well, let's look at it like this. Let's say you spend $2,500 a year on a yellow page ad, and it brings you in 100 prospective customers.

You have paid $25 for each person that has come into your store who *might* purchase from you. That is a static cost. You pay that $25 if they buy nothing from you, or if they buy everything in the store.

So what if you could increase the average transaction value of each customer by just $10? What would it cost you? Usually, nothing but a few minutes of creative thought. You've already paid $25 to get them in the store so you might as well maximize their value.

In Bob's case, he "cross-sold" them on a hot dog. It's just a matter of creatively packing complimentary goods and using the right language to get the highest number of people to say yes to buying something in addition to what they originally came in to the store to purchase.

McDonald's simply asks: "Do you want fries with that?" Extra cost for McDonald's to do that: 2 seconds of training for the employee, and 2 seconds for the employee to say it to each customer.

The result: an overall bump of about $0.08 in profit *per customer*. And when you have "over 1 billion served", that's a lot of profit!

So here's rule number 1: Spend more of your advertising budget and time on figuring out how to get customers who have purchased from you in the past, or your new prospects, to PURCHASE MORE from you.

Often times the last thing you need is more customers. Whatever problems you currently have in your business usually multiplies when you bring more customers into the funnel.

Instead, figure out how to get MORE from the same number of customers.

Which brings us to Rule Number 2: You must figure out how to get your existing customers to make more frequent purchases from you!

Here's everything required in order to make your marketing work.

- They have to KNOW you exist

- They have to want and be able to afford what you offer

- They have to trust you

You see, new customers first need to hear about you. But that's not enough. They also have to be in the market for what you offer. It's hard to sell ice cream to Eskimos.

And finally, they have to trust you enough to exchange their hard-earned dollars for the value you promise to deliver to them.

Your current customers, on the other hand, already know you exist, and have already demonstrated that they need at least some of what you offer…and at least at one point in their life they trusted you enough to exchange their dollars for the value you promised them.

All else being equal, who do you think is going to be more inclined to say yes to your next offer? A stranger -- or someone who knows you and is likely to be comfortable dealing with you again?

I think the answer is obvious. Before we go into how to get past customers to increase the frequency from which they purchase from you, let's first deal with increasing the average purchasing size from each customer.

Mistake #2: Not Effectively   Using Cross-sells, Up-sells OR "Package" Selling

We already discussed "cross sells" with the "do you want fries with that?" example. So what's this mean for your business? The first thing you need to do is implement your own cross-sells.

Here's a simple way to do that. Look at your 5 to 7 most popular sellers in your business. Each one of them should have a cross-sell. For example in the flooring business, when people buy carpeting, you should also have a special offer for them to buy "spot remover" along with their carpeting.

You can even give them a special "purchase discount" because you don't need as high a margins since you have already PAID (in marketing and advertising) to attract them to come in the door and purchase from you.

So select your five biggest sellers, and find other items that you can offer that complement these main purchases, just like fries compliment a cheeseburger.

Then, just create a quick script to use and to train your employees to use this technique. It could be something as simple as "Would you be interested in receiving a special 60% purchaser discount on spot remover to complement your flooring purchase today?"

Anything is better than nothing. Based on tests, even a weak attempt at a cross sell works 6%-20% of the time. The point being is that cross sells have almost no hard cost at all to implement, so why not do it?

The second thing is the up-sell. This is where you try to offer them a more premium version of what they are ready to purchase. Let's return to the flooring example.

There are different pads you can put under your carpet. There is the basic pad, often made of several different materials that are bonded together, thus making it cheaper to sell to the client. Then there is "prime" pad, which is solid, more durable, makes the flooring last longer, but is more expensive.

In this case, when putting together an offer for the customer, you'd want to say something like "Would you like to invest a little bit more to make this carpet last 6 years longer – and feel more comfortable under your feet?"

Then, you simply explain why buying the upgraded version of the padding is a better option for them.

Now think about it – if your markup is the same for both types of padding, then you'll make more money if you sell them the more expensive carpet pad. Example: let's say you make 50% profit on each pad you sell. If a customer needs 100 square yards of the basic pad, and that sells for $4.50 per square yard, then you just sold $450 of materials, of which $225 is profit to you.

But what if you could've bumped them up to the premium pad that sells for $7.50 per square yard? Now that's $750 in material sold, of which $375 is profit to you.

That's an increase of $150 for just a *few minutes* of sales work. Again, all you have to do is come up with a simple script, and a simple way to demonstrate why the little bit of extra cost involved for the customer is worth the investment in terms of what they're going to get for that little extra bit of cost.

So how can you make this work for you? Go back to those 5-7 popular products and simply ask yourself -- "Is there an upgraded and/or premium version of this that I can offer to my customers?"

There always is. And often times, you can *make* a premium version without hardly any additional hard cost, if you focus on *intangibles*. Let me give you an example.

Let's say you own a high-end restaurant. One premium version you can offer to your clients is the "immediate seating" club. For a small fee each year, these customers can guarantee that they get seated as soon as they enter the restaurant.

In this case, you're selling time and convenience, not a product. That has a lot of value in this day and age.

Or you could even create a special area for preferred customers that has a much more luxurious feel to it, to make them enjoy the atmosphere more. Again, you're selling luxury, not a product... another intangible.

The final sales technique you should consider using is "Packaged Selling" also known as "Bundled Offers". Most people prefer to have someone else make the decision for them, so they don't have any responsibility in the matter.

Let's return to the flooring example. Why not create an "Active Lifestyle Package". This would be for people with young children, maybe pets as well, or for those who have high traffic homes.

For this special package, you choose the carpet, padding, vinyl and tile options, and then sell it as a package, instead of each component on its own. This allows you to already INCLUDE the premium versions, or the products that have the highest profit margins.

Your customers are more likely to say yes, if you do it right, since it's easier for them to say yes.

Then, the next logical step is to up-sell them to an even more deluxe package. Ha! In this case it could be the "Active but Luxurious Lifestyle Package."

Let's go back to our restaurant example. Let's design the "Romance Package". In this case, the customer would get a limo to pick them up at their door, they get a special table near the fireplace that is more secluded, they get a vase filled with beautiful flowers that they get to take home and keep (including the vase), and they get a special "Lover's Dessert" for the lucky couple to share.

You're no longer in the restaurant business... you're in the romance business... and you can charge a lot more for that!

At the very least, you need to create one "package" that you can offer to a certain portion of your clients. Make it much higher priced and more luxurious than normal so that even if only a handful of customers say yes to it each year, you'll have made a pretty good extra bit of profits without doing hardly any more work.

Mistake #3: Not Understanding the Lifetime Value of a Customer

If you knew the potential lifetime value of even an average customer, you'd spend far more time making sure existing customers continued to use your services, and far less time trying to get new customers.

Let me give you an example. Let's say Lucy is 45 and spends $100 a week at her preferred grocery store. Lucy doesn't plan on moving any time soon, and has at least 15 more years of good shopping left in her.

So let's see, 15 years is 780 weeks. And at an average of $100 a week, that's $78,000. If you owned that grocery store, don't you think it would be prudent to come up with a strategy to make sure Lucy keeps coming back to you?

Now get this. A famous study done 20 years ago, that was recently just re-tested and re-confirmed, found out what causes people to quit going to a store or a service provider. Here are the results.

9% - Leave because of competition

OK, so someone else might come along offering them a better deal, or better service. Or perhaps they have a location that's closer than yours. It sucks, but that is part of the game. Nonetheless the instructive thing to recognize is that you *only* lose 9% of your customers because of this.

9% - Leave because they move

It's hard to get someone to come back to your store if they move halfway across the country. It's just the nature of the beast. Some will move because we are by nature nomadic creatures.

14% - Leave because of a complaint or dissatisfaction with service or product.

Okay, this can be worked on a bit, but one thing I've learned in business is you can't please everyone, nor do you want to. Anyway, it's not that big of a deal, because there is something FAR, FAR greater that causes your customers to go somewhere else.

It is greater than all these other factors combined. Here it is:

68% - Leave because of perceived apathy of the service provider.

In other words, they feel you only look at them, as a customer to get money from, and that you don't care about them. Notice the word *perceived.* You might very well care about them, but if you don't show them you care about them in a way that's unique and that isn't something that everyone else does, then there is no reason for them to remain loyal to you.

So if you don't have a specific "customer retention" strategy in place, you're losing 2/3rds of your previous customers! When you consider the potential lifetime value of a customer that should make you sick to your stomach!

So what's the remedy? First, you need to increase the amount of communication you have with your past customers. At the very least, follow the "4 a day rule". Every business day, someone in your business should contact at least 4 past customers with a personal follow up, either by email, phone, letter or in person.

You should also consider a newsletter... and no, not those fancy, beautiful and "corporate looking" newsletters I'm sure your familiar with. You need to take a more personal approach.

People don't fall in love with corporations. They fall in love with personalities. The first part of that word is "person". You have to open up to them. Let them know who you are and a little bit about what's going on in your life. You also have to show some character and a bit of humor, and style.

Think of why you're close friends with the friends you're close with. You should try to establish that same bond with your customers. There are several strategies I use to do this, i.e. with a monthly newsletter.

Finally, someone who cares about you looks out for your best interest with no ulterior motive in mind. Again, that's where a newsletter comes in handy. Each month, you can create an article giving them tips on how to better their life, improve the value they can get from your services, and just things that can make them feel better about themselves. And they're getting all this stuff just because they're a customer of yours.

That's how you make someone feel special.

At any rate, you need to create some kind of customer retention campaign, and that's often just staying in contact with past customers, once every few months to let them know you're still thinking about them.

Step 11: Relationship Marketing - Social Media.

50+ years ago, forming relationships was the core of every business. Making quality products that lasted for years, knowing people by their first names, understanding your customers needs and being an active part of the community where your customers lived was not only expected but required, if you were to be successful.

Over time, these requirements changed, businesses became far less personal and the public became far too busy to care. But customers over time, have become a little disgruntled with this lack of caring and personalization. The human condition suggests that people want to feel connected and feel that they are listened to.

Today, with the advent of the Internet and the ability to communicate far more effectively and quicker than ever before, social media is now here and it's here to stay. Social media/marketing isn't a totally new concept, but how we use it is. Social media/marketing just does not cover or do justice for what is required in today's marketing. Which is why we prefer to call it Relationship Marketing.

WHAT IS RELATIONSHIP MARKETING AND HOW DOES IT WORK?

Since you already identified your target market, you're already one step ahead of the game. Now you need to figure out where your target market interacts online. This is the first key part of building your relationship marketing strategy. This step is where you begin to more fully Integrate Online Marketing Tactics and take them to a whole new level.

The Referral Marketing Goldmine

The power of "Word of Mouth"

Referrals are the cheapest, yet the most effective marketing in the world.

The idea is that you should be generating a large portion of your new customers by marketing to existing customers.

There are several reasons why this is smart to do. First, quality attracts quality. Psychologists say that you are basically a combination of your five closest friends. In other words, people will refer people who are similar to them.

So if you have a big spender, then guess what? They'll probably refer other big spenders. Every good customer should be actively pursued for a referral because they'll usually generate other customers of equal quality and value.

Also, marketing is usually met with skepticism. That's because you are often tooting your horn. But what if some one else was tooting your horn for you?

Know this – people are more likely to believe in you if someone else endorses your quality than if you yourself brag about your own qualities.

What you're really doing is leveraging off of someone else's credibility. People who take the recommendations of their friends are now coming to you with a preconceived notion that you're *already* quality – before you even have to open your mouth.

Finally word of mouth marketing is target marketing. Basically, you're only going to be getting people who already are in the market for what you're offering. Mass marketing does not have this effect. If you run an ad on television, you're getting everybody who watches TV.

But with referral marketing, you're pretty much *only* getting people who are already great matches to your products or services. This means your closing rate will go up without having to learn one single bit of salesmanship. You're just getting people who are already more likely to say "yes" before they even enter into the store.

Okay, know my rule of thumb when it comes to referral marketing – every good customer should get three direct chances to refer someone else to you.

I have found in order to get the best results, you have to ask someone three times to make a referral on your behalf. If you do nothing else, you should do this.

However, to really make it effective, there are two more things you need to do: make it easy for them to refer, and make it worthwhile to refer. I'm going to show you how to do all of this and more, as I outline what I have found time and time again to be a profit-pulling monster when it comes to referral systems.

The Referral System, Step by Step

First, get your metrics in order. How much money can you afford to spend on marketing for next month? Whatever it is, devote the largest portion of it to your referral marketing. So step one, find your budget.

Now, the specific plan I'm going to lay out to you is going to cost around $8 per person to perform. So if you have a budget of $800 for marketing, then you can reach 100 people.

Start small and scale up – that's my advice. Don't spend too much upfront until you get back some reliable figures, and you can do some testing. Since this is a system, every dollar you spend will be tracked and traced back to determine the return on investment.

Here's how it works. Someone comes in and buys from you. Immediately the next day, you send them out a letter in the mail. You thank them, ask for the referral, make it easy for them to refer, and then make it worth their while. If possible, send them both an email message and an actual letter.

The most important part here is that it's in *their* best interest to refer others to you. For that to happen, first and foremost you must have provided quality and value. So I'm going to assume you're performing good service and living up to your end of the deal.

Second, gifts work wonders. My favorite kind of gifts are those that either cost me nothing or very little, but have a huge perception of value.

Without a doubt, there is one gift I can consistently create for basically nothing, and it always does the trick.

Coupon Books

It works like this – you go around to different business owners and tell them that you want to make sure your customers shop locally. As a thank you gift for your customers, you'd like to give them coupons or special offers from other local merchants, so you're providing your customers with value, and also keeping business local.

Then you simply ask them if they have any coupons or anything they'd like to contribute to your "customer gift book".

Almost every business owner you talk to will take you up on this. Why? Well, most businesses are not good at marketing, and to make up for it they always have a special going on, or are willing to do anything if it means getting a few more customers in the store.

Besides, you only need to get like 15 or 20 different coupons anyway to make a great gift book. You can get this all done in a few hours.

So now you have a great gift that you can give to anybody who sends a referral your way. How much did it cost you? Just the cost to print up the coupons and mail them. So you just made a gift of high perceived value (everybody loves coupons!) that costs you about $1 to create and a few hours of sweat equity, thus, it's worth their while.

Now let's take a look at what the first referral letter should look like:

Dear Jane Customer,

The other day you made a purchase from our store, and we just wanted to say thank you from the bottom of our hearts for doing business with us. If there is anything you ever need in the future, please do not hesitate to call us up and ask. We'll see what we can do!

You may not know it, but the lifeline of our business comes from referrals. If you happen to know anyone else who could use our services, I'd be extremely happy to sit down and talk with them to see if we might be able to help them in any way.

And, if it so happens that the person you refer becomes our customer, then as a token of my appreciation I will send you my special "valued customer gift book", which has a total of over $250 off coupons for discounts from local business of all kinds!

I'll give the same gift to your friend as well.

It's really easy to refer someone to us. I've enclosed two of my business cards with your name written on the back of them. Just give them to anyone who you think could use our services. Just have them present the business card when they come in, so we know it was you that referred them!

Anyway, I just wanted to say thanks again for deciding to go with us!

Thanks,
Bob Business Owner

There is a lot of psychology that is going on in this first letter that I don't want you to miss.

First, it's personal and it's sincere. How many businesses have you bought something from in the last sixty days that sent you a personal thank you letter in the mail?

Hmmm...maybe 1 or 2 you say?

So imagine what kind of impact that your letter has when it lands in your customer's mailbox. Big impact. It says you care. Do you know why most people leave a service provider?

A few die. Some move away. Others leave because of an unresolved complaint. A handful will be stolen away by a competitor. Now add all those up, and guess what?

It usually only comes to 32% of all total customers who leave you. So what about the other 68%?

They leave simply because you never have taken the time to recognize them as something more than a customer.

Pop quiz – If you had an unresolved complaint, a direct competitor in your store trying to steal your customer, or the opportunity to let someone who purchased from you know you care... and you can only choose one option... which one should you choose?

You better choose the third option because roughly only 9% leave because of competition, and only 14% leave because of unresolved complaints.

If you do nothing else but keep in contact with your past customers and treat them as your friends and acknowledge them once in a while, you'll be putting the "golden handcuffs" on 2/3 of your customers, so you can keep selling to them again and again.

If you get nothing else out of the referral letter, you will get that personal communication that will separate you from 90% of all businesses, and almost every single one of your competitors.

The second thing that letter does is conveys your expectations. You expect all of your customers to refer. Most people don't refer simply because they don't know you want them to refer. In fact, I've had customers come up and tell my clients -- "Heck, I thought you already had enough customers... I didn't know you could take on more..."

You should've seen that business owner slap his fore-head.

Once people know that you want them to refer, you automatically increase the chances they *will* refer...even if it isn't immediate. Again, I've had people hold on to business cards for two or three years before they gave one to someone else.

Also, notice the casual tone of the letter. People prefer doing business with friends, and not faceless corporations.

Finally, it shows you care. The above letter basically says, "Hey, I know you're busy and I know you got to look out for your own self interests. That's why I've gone the extra mile to make it in your own self interest to refer to me."

Ideally, you don't want to take the above letter word for word. You want to fill in "our services" with your actual services and so forth. But I give you permission to take most of the above verbatim and use it.

But don't stop there. After the first letter one is sent out... wait 10-15 days. If you haven't gotten a referral from them yet, then send them letter two.

Dear Jane Customer,

A few weeks ago I sent you a letter thanking you for your purchase. I hope you got everything you wanted out of it and more. Remember – if you ever need help with anything, I'm only a phone call away.

We've also sent out several "customer gift books" in the last few weeks to our valued customers who referred one of their friends to us.

I know things can get busy, and sometimes stuff can get misplaced in the shuffle. To make sure you don't miss out on your own special customer gift book, I've sent you two more business cards with your name on the back – just in case you misplaced the last two I sent you.

Just give those to a friend in need, if you think we can help them, and we'll mail you your "customer gift book" pronto!

Once again, I just wanted to say thanks for being our customer, and we hope that we can continue to provide you with more service in the years to come.

Thanks,

Bob Business Owner

Here's what I know about marketing – one-shot advertising is not very effective. It's not that people don't want to act on your offers. A lot of them do. What happens is that the day to day details take over, and what they intend on doing ends up getting pushed to the back of their mind.

What this letter does is thank them again, puts you in front of them again, and basically let's them off the hook – hey, it wasn't their fault. You know they're busy people!

Also, it gives you another excuse to send them two more business cards. It also offers some social proof "hey, everybody else is referring".

Every time we track these campaigns, we usually find something like this – we get 3% to refer off the first letter. We get 4% to refer off the second letter, and we get 2% to refer off the third. In any case, all mailings are profitable.

Now think – if we just stopped after the first time, we'd get a 3% response. But instead we got a 9% response! In most scenarios, it almost always plays out that the second letter will work the best. Who knows why – it just does.

Now those who didn't respond to letter number one, and don't respond to letter number two, will get, after 10-15 more days, the third and last letter:

Dear Jane Customer,

Hope everything is going great for you! The reason I'm writing to you today is because I had a few "customer gift books" left over and didn't want them to go to waste.

I had one specifically set aside for you, so I have enclosed it with this letter. It is just our way of saying thanks for being a great customer.

Also, just in case you lost the last cards in the laundry or something, I've put in two more business cards with your name on the back.

Just pass them on to a friend if they're ever in need of any of the services that we offer…We'll make sure to treat them right.

Thanks!

Bob Business Man

Now, I don't want you to confuse the technique with the strategy. This works because:

- It puts you in front of them 3 times.

- It conveys the expectation that they will refer.

- It is personal and friendly.

- It is easy to do.

- It is in their own best interest.

You don't have to do the coupon gift book. Sometimes I'll just purchase tickets for a special upcoming local event, or even complimentary dinners at a good restaurant. There are literally dozens of ways you can incentive them.

Lastly, a few more pointers – make your letters look like personal letters. This means, when you design the layout, don't put some fancy "brochure" feel into it. Just picture how you'd design the letter if you were going to sit down and write someone a personal note from a typewriter.

Also, when you get this system in place, you'll get some numbers. You might find for every 5 customers you do this for, you get 1 referral in the next 30 days. Okay, do that math – let's say your average sale netted you $600 in profit.

And let's say when you deduct all marketing expenses for creating and mailing the letters, it cost you $100. That's a 6 to 1 return on investment! Try getting that with other types of advertising.

This type of marketing also allows you to test. What would happen if you altered the gift? You can literally test every element you want, and know what is working and what isn't working. This means you can figure out the exact combination of steps for getting the greatest return on investment.

One more point. What is great about this system, is because mobile marketing has really taken off, as we have discussed already, we can combine these strategies with other forms of online, video, and mobile marketing. When you create the right plan, and then integrate everything you do offline, with what you do online, then the impact of these tactics are intensified as much as 3 or 4 times and possibly even more.

Step 12: Relationship Marketing - Customer Service.

Continue to develop relationships in your relationship-marketing plan. People expect and want excellent customer service. A big difference between the expectations of today and that of 50+ years ago is we have fostered generations of instant gratification. People aren't always willing to wait for the type of customer service they expect.

What is your plan to provide quality customer service, in a speedy but effective manner?

People are less loyal these days to brand names than they may have once been. But they still respond well to excellent service and have a tendency to maintain loyalty, when the product or service is something they want or need and that company offers better than excellent customer service.

In addition, smaller businesses have an advantage, as more and more people prefer to do business locally. Large corporations may be able to provide a price incentive, but depending on the industry, they may not always provide the type of relationships your customers might expect. As a small business, you need to provide something your customers can't get from the Big Corporations.

You may need to provide them something they don't even know they want yet. You might be a small business, but in your community, you are very important.

Relationship Marketing is the Capstone of all your Marketing efforts; it is what all your marketing efforts should focus towards accomplishing. You may have noticed how most of the steps prior to these last two steps, all involved building some kind of relationship. Whether it was with your employees, contractors or customers, everything ends up being about the relationships you create and how you maintain them.

My goal in creating the Relationship Marketing Model, which helps you combat Praeconititus, the prevalent disease of wasting your marketing dollars, has been in an effort to build a relationship with you and your business.

Anyone that tells you that you can have instant results or if they say just buy this one thing and everything will be perfect, first off run, and run really fast!

If they show you how to advertise, but neglect the other parts of your planning or basically they do anything that neglects or does not even consider any of the 12 steps found in the Relationship Marketing Model, then they are not being honest or fair with you or your business.

There are specialists or 'experts' in many of the areas that make up the Relationship Marketing Model, these specialists know and do an amazing job and as you know from step one, are even necessary to achieving success in your marketing and business. We even use professionals such as these. But if you're not planning and taking into account all these areas, then ultimately, no matter how good those specialists are, you are probably still just wasting money that could be more effectively used someplace else.

Make sure that that they and you are asking the right questions.

Having a business can and should be a wonderful, rewarding and profitable venture, but it does take time and effort to effectively implement all the proper steps and there is NO 'One Size Fits All' Solution. There is no instant success guaranteed solution. There is no perfect business and there certainly is no get rich quick business without some work and effort on your part. Believe me, I wish any one of them were.

Don't be another statistic; be a success, you now have the cure to Praeconititus. You can stop wasting your marketing and advertising dollars today by doing the simple things found in this book and when you are ready, finding a Relationship Marketing Coach to help you effectively implement into your business each of the steps found within the **Relationship Marketing Model**.

Oh wait, there's just one more chapter, to really help wrap things up.

Tearing Down Customer Resistance

How many of the people who walk into your business, or who take an interest in your products and services, end up going ahead with a purchase? In sales, this is called a closing rate.

To manage something, you first have to measure it. That way you know where it's at, so you know what you need to do to improve it.

So here's a simple question you need to have an answer to – if 10 prospects are interested in doing business with you, on average how many out of those 10 end up doing business with you?

The percentage itself isn't important. In stores with a lot of traffic, you can do 1 out of 10 and be fine. I have friends with websites where they do 1 out of 100, and it's good enough for them to make a great return on investment, because it takes hardly any time or effort. In some businesses, you need 5 out of 10 just to have a chance at making a profit.

What *is* important is knowing how to improve your percentages to a more "acceptable" range. So if you get 5 out of 10, do the math and see how much more you'd make if you got 6 out of 10. Since they're already coming in the door, most of the work is done. You're just looking for those "little things" to get more people converted into customers.

There are a lot of different ways to improve your closing rate, and some are more complicated than others. I always look for the "80/20" factor in any given task. In other words

I'm looking for that one or two key things that will make most of the difference between someone purchasing from you or not. Here's some insight to help you discover that "vital one fact" that gives you a majority of your results.

Do you know what three things are *required* before a prospect becomes a customer? Knowing this will give you the answer you need. Here are the three things that are needed:

1. First, they have to want what you offer.

2. Second, they have to have money to purchase it.

3. Third, they have to believe that you'll actually come through on your end of the deal.

The more inclined they are to already want what you have, the easier it is to sell to them. The more money they have set aside for making consumer purchases, the easier it is to sell to them. The more they believe that you actually will deliver on your offer, the easier it is to sell to them.

Because it is my favorite place to go to learn what NOT to do when writing ads, I have before me a phone book with yellow page ads. I'm going to flip through it and quote some phrases. Here are just a few (*and the thoughts*):

- **"Dependable & Quality Service"**

  And here's what your typical savvy potential customer is thinking:

  "Oh yeah!? Says who?"

- **"Value, Service & Convenience"**

This description is meaningless, and everybody knows it… They're thinking:

"Prove It!"

- **"Friendly service"**

Once again, consumers have heard this all before, and they are thinking:

"Yeah, right!

In other words, these are hollow phrases of puffery that everybody uses. It's so easy to say those things, and so saying those things mean very little. I've actually called a business whose yellow page ad said "friendly service" only to be treated rudely by the receptionist who answered the phone. Guess someone forgot to tell her!

So how do you go beyond mere puffery and actually prove your case that you're friendlier, more valuable, offer better service and are more dependable than every other option they have available?

Well, I'll share with you one simple way to do this that will drastically differentiate you from every competitor, both direct and indirect. As a bonus, it's also very simple to do, is extremely cost effective and when compiled, can be used in a variety of different outlets and mediums. What I'm talking about is customer testimonials.

The Selling Power of Testimonials

If you want to increase your closing rates without resorting to any fancy tricks or learning a bunch of new skills, just start being an avid collector of testimonials.

I don't care what anyone else says, they work.

Consider this – what if I told you I was the greatest marketing consultant of all time? Would you really believe me? What if your friend called you up and told you I was the greatest marketing consultant? Then you *might* believe it.

But what if your lawyer, your doctor, your mother, your children's principal, the head of your trade association and the guy you buy peaches from at the local farmer's market told you I was the greatest marketing consultant of all time?

I bet you'd be really interested in sitting down and having a talk with me, wouldn't you? You'd probably think a great deal more of me compared to how you'd feel if I just called you up and started bragging about my skills.

This is such a simple principle; it makes me wonder – why don't *all* businesses use testimonials? I don't know why. I think it should be a requirement of doing business personally. That is because, when it comes to raising your closing rates, it makes all the difference.

Now let me show you when, where and how to get these killer testimonials that will increase the believability of your offers.

How to Become an Avid Testimonial Collector

If you go looking for opportunities to get testimonials, you'll find it's easy to begin collecting them.

The best opportunity is when your customer is "in heat". What I mean by this is that you've just done something that has "wowed" them. They might come in to pay their bill and say "I can't believe what a wonderful service you did. It's better than the last five people I've gone to!"

This is your chance! You say: "Thanks! Would it be okay if I shared your story with others who might be interested in our services as well? It really helps us better serve our clients!"

Or, you can say: "Thanks. Would it be okay if I wrote down what you just said and shared it with others? It would mean a lot to me!" Then just write down really quickly what was said, and have them approve it.

Or you can simply say: "Thanks. Did you know that one of the best ways we get good clients just like you is sharing the success stories of our past clients? Would it be okay if we quoted you in some of our marketing and sales communications?"

Don't make it harder than it has to be. The main process is – get them when they're in a good mood. Ask if you can have their permission to quote them and share their story. Then get their testimonial. That's it.

Also, it's smart if you ask them if you can share their name with others as well, just to be on the safe side.

If you do nothing else, just collect testimonials from customers who are in heat and have just expressed how appreciative they are of you and your services.

Another good time is when you "save the day". Did you do something for a customer that was out of the ordinary? Maybe you made a house call at 8:30 at night to fix an emergency, free of charge. Or perhaps they wanted something that was supposedly discontinued, but you went the extra mile and tracked down what they were looking for.

Anytime you save the day, just ask them for a testimonial. In fact, I intentionally look for opportunities to save the day, because it serves in my self-interest. If I go the extra mile, then I know they'll give me one heck of a testimonial! This is the power of reciprocity at work. They feel as though they owe you and because we always want things to be right with the world or in balance, we find ways to reciprocate.

Once you get good at the first two, consider sending out a customer survey once in a while. Have them answer a few key questions. Then, retype those answers up in letter form, and ask them to sign off on it as a testimonial that you can share with others.

There are more aggressive ways to get testimonials, and I would encourage you to be aggressive about getting them, especially after you've gotten the knack for getting the low hanging fruit. Once you get used to asking your "in heat customers" and those who you've "saved the day for", experiment with actively seeking out testimonials to further prove your case.

How to Use Testimonials for Maximum Effect

I'm going to give you some examples that you can literally knock off and use in your own business, and also that you can use to brainstorm your own ideas from.

Let's return to the yellow book example. Instead of the typical puffery, your ad might include something that says:

"Look, any business can say that they care about the customer and that they are dependable and have high quality service. Instead of us touting our own horn, maybe you'd rather hear it from some of our customers themselves. Just call our 'satisfied customer hot line' to hear a pre-recorded message of what our customers think about our services..."

You know how much a voice mail account costs? For free if you look in the right places, but otherwise it is about $4 a month. For $4 a month, you can have a recording of your best customers. How do you get these recordings?

Here are a few ideas.

Perhaps you have your sales reps call your customers a few days after the sale. Explain to the customer that for quality issues, would it be okay if you recorded the call? This can be done inexpensively with a digital phone recorder that costs less than $50, or through an online service for about $10 a month.

Then, ask your customer what their thoughts were on the service or for the product. At the end, ask them if it would be okay if you shared their thoughts with others who might be interested in the products or services.

That's just one way to ask for your testimonials and then getting them recorded. There are others. For instance here are a few more options for recording testimonials.

It is just as easy to get a VOIP (*Voice Over Internet Protocol*) PBX phone system. What is VOIP, it's just an acronym for a phone that uses the internet instead of a traditional landline. You can get a quality one for about $25 a month and they have the ability to record conversations. Some VOIP voicemail systems even have the ability to post voice messages directly online, so people can listen to them.

Another option, for recording testimonials is to set up a dedicated extension or line, to collect them. With a VOIP PBX style phone system, you should be able to designate an extension to a voicemail box that does nothing but collects them.

Or you can use Google. That's right, currently, as of the date of this publication, for no cost at all, you can set up a Google Voice phone number, that allows you to embed voicemails left in your mailbox, anywhere you wish.

With any of these other options, you can either ask customers to leave messages for you or you can three-way them into the system right on the spot and have them leave you a quick testimonial.

Now you have a tool – you have people talking about how good you are. You can put this prerecorded message into all of your marketing communications! Your believability goes through the roof.

Here's something else you might want to consider – gathering up a "testimonial book".

Do you know ANY salesperson who has a testimonial book? Hmm... Wouldn't that distinguish you from every other competitor out there? I think it would... and in a good way.

Let's say you really went the extra mile and totally knock it out of the park for a customer. They were so happy they called you up and thanked you personally, and said they were so impressed with you and that you went above and beyond the call of duty.

Well how about this – you ask them if it would be okay to feature them as "case study" in your next advertisement. Then you could write an advertisement that looks like an article, where you simply tell the story of what you did for this customer. This type of advertisement is about a million times more effective than "BUY MY PRODUCT!" advertisements you currently see everywhere.

At the very least, you should include some testimonials in your advertising, just to enhance your claims.

Several people I know have gone as far as recording on video their customer testimonials. Then one in particular, what he would do is when someone doesn't purchase the first time they came into his store, five days later they'd get the video in the mail or by email, that contained all these wonderful customer testimonials.

Needless to say, a lot of people came back and ended up purchasing who otherwise would not have.

The Anatomy of a Good Testimonial

Now, some people have tried testimonials and have told me that they don't work. Well, it reminds me of my friends Dad telling me several years ago that his DVD player didn't work. I asked him -- "Did you plug it in?"

Oops!

Testimonials are like anything else – if you do them poorly then they probably won't work. In order to do them right, you must know what a good testimonial looks like.

Here's a bad testimonial:

"You did a good job!"

Here's a killer testimonial:

"You responded to our call and were at our house in 7 minutes. The last guys took 2 hours. Not only that, you helped us save 13% off the cost. Thanks a bunch!" -- Johnny Gratitude, Fire Fighter, Portland, OR

The difference is obvious. Bad testimonials are bland and really don't say anything. Good testimonials are specific, and give you hard facts. I love it when someone says to me: "I read your book on Thursday, and by Saturday morning I did one thing I learned on page 8 that resulted in me making $14,967.12 in profit by the following Tuesday. You're a genius!".

That's a far better testimonial than "your ideas helped me make more money".

Not only is specificity needed, but it's good to have a name, location, and occupation. Otherwise people will think that maybe you're just making up the testimonials yourself, even though that is illegal. (*Which is why audio and video testimonials are the best*)

Also, there are other things that can influence your testimonials. What's better – five testimonials featured in your ads from white males aged 43 and over, or a mix of ages, races and both males and females?

Well, it depends. If your product targets white males that are 43 years old, then it's a good idea. If it targets a wide variety of audiences, then you want testimonials from a wide variety of people.

Lastly, as humans we're hardwired by nature to trust authority. That's why testimonials from scientists, doctors, nurses, fire fighters, and other esteemed positions tend to have more pull than regular testimonials. Even Celebrities have this same effect, which is why so many companies use them. Although it is important to note that there are some controversial issues surrounding some Celebrity Endorsements.

When it comes to true testimonials from anyone that is famous, an authority figure, and credible that has actually used your product or service, they do work. But authentic testimonials are more valuable than any paid celebrity endorsement, hands down. Just think how much more credible a testimonial is from a rocket scientist than a "sanitary engineer", unless your business happens to involve product or services that are related to what a "sanitary engineer" happens to do.

So set a plan – come up with the different ways you're going to capture and use testimonials, and make sure everybody in your business starts to become a testimonial collector. It's one of the easiest ways to increase your sales closing percentage.

Glossary

[1] Here is an easy way to distinguish and understand the differences between these three types of plans:

- **Business Plan**
  Your business plan is an overall, strategic map. It provides the foundation for every thing your business does. Generally business plans don't change very much or very often. They do need to be reviewed and understood, usually at least once every couple of years, but they aren't typically the day-to-day action plan necessary for success.

- **Marketing Plan**
  Your marketing plan is the action portion of your planning. This is how you will accomplish each portion of your business plan. Where you will spend your money, the metrics that you use to measure successes and failures; it's the how and who of your planning process. All marketing plans must be flexible enough to change, but unlike an advertising plan, they won't typically change on a daily basis. Marketing plans are both tactical and strategic in nature, but they are always based on action.

- **Advertising Plan**
  Your advertising plan on the other hand is the most tactical type of plan, it's the pinpointed way you will let people know about your business, it's how you will find new employees and as mentioned it is very fluid and targeted for specific purposes. Advertising plans will come and go with many, many different purposes.

Many see advertising, as the fun part of your business, and it is very results driven.

Because your advertising plan may be the most visible part of your business, it will often get far more attention, while at the same time potentially being the biggest source of waste for your bottom line. Avoid Praeconititus and "Shotgun Marketing". Don't skimp on the other plans, just so you can throw more dollars at this one.

[2] Literally speaking:

'Prae' is really the root of praereptor...or Thief.
'Con' is really the root of consexus...or Gullible.

Yes, Praeconititus is a word that we [a business partner and I] just made up, to illustrate a point.

Testimonials

Justin has been a wealth of knowledge and personal help to me in my marketing business. He has the ability to see things in a different light and present alternative options to a sitaution. It's great to have someone who understands what you do to provide additional insight. He is genuine and ready and willing to help.

I am looking forward to seeing what he has up his sleeve next.

Lesley Howe
Owner Firecracker Marketing & Promotions
Flint, MI

I have had the opportunity to mastermind with Justin on a number of occasions, and Justin truly is a visionary thinker. Not only does he help to validate my ideas or provide perspective to them, but he has also helped me to formulate new ideas that have helped me with clients and my own business. Any time you work with Justin, you know you will get honest straight-forward opinions and ideas. There are not two many people whose opinions I truly take to heart. However, Justin is one person whose opinions are always taken seriously.

Ray Lane
Ohm Media
www.marketingthathitsohm.com

The old adage "It's not what you know but who you know" - can be appled to Justin. Justin regularly contributes information to friends and colleagues, building a deep realtionship with many people, which will result in his being top of mind for projects and assistance. It's great knowing Justin.

Graeme Nichol, CEO
Arcturus Advisors,
Jacksonville FL

Justin is very knowledgeable and extremely talented when it comes to social media marketing. His willingness to give value to his friends, colleagues and clients proves his character is that of a true long term thinker and business associate. Dilligent, persistent, and a true thought leader in the online space.

Cassiah Jay
Dallas, Texas

"Justin Taylor is a person I go to when I need help with SEO, internet marketing, social media marketing, mobile marketing or if I have questions regarding Google Apps and Google+. He has the answer to basically any question I have. Justin is always there to help, he is a giving person and his solutions are invaluable to my business. If you want to learn about Relationship Marketing , then The Relationship Marketing Model is an up to date informative source. I read it from cover to cover non-stop. It is no fluff, high value content. Just grab your copy and read it, you won't be sorry!"

Galina Vitols
U2 Marketing
www.small-business-marketing-101.com

I have had the fortune and pleasure to work with Justin in many social media and internet marketing projects. Justin has been an invaluable resource with his expertise and his willingness to share his experience and knowledge with others. Not only does Justin have a deep understanding of social media platforms and is on the forefront of learning new technology, he also exhibits strong leadership qualities and is always ready to help and coach his peers, clients, and colleagues. I am also a member of Justin's online marketing mastermind group and whenever there is a complex problem or question, Justin always takes the initiative and applies his strategic thinking to help figure out a sound solution. I feel very honored to know and work with Justin and he would be a valuable asset for anyone seeking to take their business to the next level through his marketing strategies.

Laura DeMeo
laura@laurademeo.com
http://www.linkedin/in/laurademeo (laurademeo@yahoo.com)
www.laurademeo.com

Thank you for all your free coaching advice and helpful insights on how to appropriately build an online marketing business. As a newbie to this field, everything seems a bit overwhelming and can create information overload, but you have managed to give some great recommendations and solutions for our many queries. Your advise has been simple and very easy to follow and incorporate and although I am no way at your level yet, I do hope that you continue to assist us in whichever way that you can.

Thank you and I wish you all the best with the book launch.

Best wishes,
Sophia Spence
Kainos Concepts Consulting Ltd
Email: sspence@kainosconcepts.com

Justin Taylor and I crossed paths about 6 months ago and all I can say is: Wow.

Seldom have I had the privilege of meeting someone who is extremely intense, giving and knowledgable in his fields of expertise. In this case it is marketing in the onlines ector for offline businesses.

His dedication to thoroughness and his drive to understand concepts has truly allowed him to emerge as a leader in the networking group where I have come to appreciate his input -- basically on a daily basis!

Contrary to many who are quick to give answers and solutions, Justin really has tried his methods and I know that I can take his answers for face value, trust that they will work or discuss some of the hiccups I may come across due to the specifics to my own issues.

Justin is always willing to help out and is therefore an inspiration to me: you reap what you sow. Even observing how he generously helps others (on issues which may not be problematic for me) give testimony to what it means to offer true value to the community.

If you are looking for a true giver to the community, then keep your eyes out for this book and future publications, I am confident that Justin Taylor will not disappoint you.

Andrea Schmitz
http://schmitz-academy.info/

Justin Taylor is one of the most giving guys online. He is always there to help out and he has helped me out many times over. Justin is very knowledgeable when it comes to online marketing and shares his knowledge freely and with great gusto. I am grateful for all of the things I have learned from this talented man.

Robin Buckley
Lake Oswego, OR
Robin Buckley Photography
http://RobinBuckley.com
http://PacificSocialMedia.com/

Justin Taylor is a treasure chest of knowledge. I've never met Justin in person, but I do follow his posts. Usually I can a get one or two gold nuggets from his contributions that either point me in the right direction or help me stay the course. Justin is a "goto" guy and gives without strings attached. In this day and age that is a rare find. Keep up the good work Justin!

Brian Jones
www.KrushItOnlineMarketing.com

About the Author

Author, consultant, and online marketing pro. Justin Taylor is an expert at idea generation and overcoming difficult obstacles. Justin is a Life and Marketing coach, specializing in Online Marketing.

Justin has a Bachelor of Science Degree in Marketing and a Bachelor of Science Degree in Advertising Management. Justin also has an MBA in Marketing and currently pursuing a PhD. in Organizational Leadership.

Justin is a lifelong learner, an Entrepreneur, and co-founder of several businesses. Justin is an enrolled member of the Confederated Tribes of Grand Ronde.

Justin is the creator of the Relationship Marketing Model and can help you implement the principles of the Relationship Marketing Model and/or help you get certified as a Relationship Marketing Model Coach. Justin is a specialist at helping small businesses gain a dominant position in their local marketplace.

Justin specializes in helping entrepreneurs and small businesses gain a competitive advantage in both their on and offline marketing. He makes sure that these businesses are able to be "found" on the internet, ensures that they never run out of leads, and helps them to transform these potential clients into lifetime customers (*and raving fans!*).

If you are serious about improving your own business' bottom line, and would like to schedule a free consultation to see how Justin or one of his team members can create a comprehensive on and/or offline marketing campaign for your company, just point your mobile telephone or your computer to his website www.JustinTaylor.tel where you will find his most up to date phone, email, social media contacts, and/or other links to more information.